M000112325

Frankie

At Home in the Kitchen

Frankie's Pizza & Pasta

Easy Italian recipes to make at home

By Frank Curtiss

Frankie's Food & Wine Publishing

Library of Congress Cataloging-in-Publication Data

Curtiss, Frank.

Frankie at home in the kitchen./Frank Curtiss—1st ed.
p. cm.

ISBN 9780983113102

1. Cooking. 2. Italian recipes. I. Title.

Library of Congress Control Number: 2011921676

Published by Frankie's Food & Wine Publishing,
11744 158th Avenue NE, Redmond, Washington 98052
USA,   Telephone 425-269-3909
frankpizza@aol.com

Distributed to the book trade through Independent
Publishers Group (IPG) by Wild River Press, Post Office
Box 13360, Mill Creek, Washington 98082 USA

Wild River Press Web site address:
www.wildriverpress.com

Printed in Hong Kong through Global Interprint

10 9 8 7 6 5 4 3 2 1

Table of Contents

A few words from Frankie

A cook book is merely a collection of recipes. But I desire to give you more than that. My wish is to impart a love of life, and the joy of loving and being loved by the God who created you and blessed you.

One of his greatest gifts to us is food. It nourishes our bodies. Yet I believe that he meant it to be more than that. When prepared and shared with love and a grateful heart, it feeds our soul as well.

What better place to share life with family and friends than around the table. And yet even our quiet moments of dining alone can delight our souls if we remember that we are partaking of his goodness.

It would give me great joy to know that I had contributed to the richness of that experience. And even greater joy if I somehow created a touch-point between you and the God who reaches down to you. For remember, "Man does not live by bread alone, but by every word that comes from the mouth of God".

May your table overflow with wonderful food, laughter and love.

Frankie

Thanks and Aknowledgements

There have been so many people who've assisted me with this project; with everything from preparing food, to food photography, to testing recipes, to proof reading.

I had more recipe testers than I will be able to list, but I want them all to know that I am forever grateful for their support. I could not have accomplished this without their help.

I'd like to thank my friend, Janine Wilson, for assisting with proof reading the introduction to my book.

As for the photography, I had assistance from highly skilled amateurs and professionals alike. Early in this project, we conducted a food shoot at our home, and a second shoot at a "cook book party" held in the home of our good friends, Brad and Mary Beth Cecil. Through these, Laurie Ascanio, Brad Cecil, and Mike Craddock contributed some beautiful photos, with the assistance of Mary Beth Cecil who did the food styling. Other friends, Rick and Jean Curtin, Lisa and Bruce Jarrard, and Ron and Cathie Barnhart helped with food preparation, washing dishes, and generally creating joviality. These people are all dear friends with whom we have celebrated life, death, food, wine and a love of all things Italian.

In addition to that, there were two couples, professionals in the photography business, who contributed their services. The first, Mark and Diane Kulp, did some in-restaurant shooting to provide us a stock of photos from which to draw for this book and our web-site. They also shot the gorgeous family portrait shown a couple of pages hence. The second couple was Doug and MaryAnn Adams (dougadamsstudio.com), who provided beautiful shots of two of our pizzas. Tante grazie to the four of you!

There is another gentleman I'd like to thank who came into my life during this project. That is Thomas Pero of Wild River Press. Tom unselfishly helped steer my project with sound advice. And as a result I have chosen to team up with him to distribute this book on a national basis.

I want to note three people at the restaurant who made noteable contributions. The first is my chef, Andy Rafferty (photo, page 70), who helped me in taking many of our large restaurant recipes and breaking them down to "human size". This often involved going shopping to see what sizes of products were available at the grocery store, and then re-working and re-testing recipes. The other two were my pasta chef, Jirina, a fourteen year veteran with us, who prepared most of the beautiful pasta dishes for my food shoots; and my son Noah who did the same for so many of my pizza shoots. They are both artists with food!

One couple in particular I'd like to thank are our friends Ron and Cathie Barnhart. Ron and Cathy lived in Umbria for a year and have imparted to me much inspiration, passion and insight on Italian food and culture. In addition to testing many of my recipes at their home, Ron also came to my house multiple times to assist me in testing new recipes. For myself, those were some the most enjoyable times on this project. I think Ron had fun also.

And most importantly, I'd like to thank my family. Especially my wife Rhonda who has been a tremendous support. She's put up with numerous kitchen messes, late dinners, cold food (after I've photographed it), and time I've stolen from her to peck away at my computer. She is amazing!

Photo shoots with friends

Brad Cecil and Laurie Ascanio

Mike Craddock

Jean Curtin

Rick Curtin (AKA Ricco)

Frankie

Cathie Barnhart

Pasta with Sardines

Brad Cecil (AKA Bradolini)

Mary Beth Cecil

Ron Barnhart (AKA Ronaldo)

Busy hands

Bruce and Lisa Jarrard

About Frankie's:

People often ask how I came up with the idea of Frankie's. I explain that I designed a place that I would like to eat at and hoped others would too. I longed for a little neighborhood place where my family and I would know the customers and they knew us. What resulted of that dream was a small, casual Italian cafe serving in pizza and pasta located in the downtown area of the friendly town of Redmond, Washington.

Frankie's is our baby. We are a family owned and operated restaurant; opened by my wife Rhonda and I in 1993, with the help of our two oldest sons, Chris and Noah. When their two younger siblings, Joel and Jenna, came of age, they too came to work at the restaurant. Not long after we were joined by our daughter-in-law, Chris's wife Sandra. It is truly a family business. Today, our oldest son Chris is our manager, though Rhonda and I are still involved in day-to-day operations. Our son Noah is our head pizza chef; and our daughter, Jenna, who is in the Army Reserve, recently returned to work for us after serving a year in Iraq.

We call Frankie's "your friendly neighborhood Italian cafe" which we feels aptly describes who we are. We've somehow resisted the pressure to expand. We enjoy working together and having just one restaurant allows us to have the hands-on touch we desire, while still maintaining a good quality of life for all of us.

From the beginning we looked to fill a niche between an everyday pizza joint and your white tablecloth Italian dining. It appears we've found the spot. Since our inception, we've been blessed with excellent business. Plan on waiting for a table when you come in.

We make nearly everything from scratch at Frankie's; from our pizza and bread dough to our sauces, soups, desserts, and salad dressings. We even make our own sausage. Our pizza is made in a New York style with both traditional and gourmet toppings, baked in a traditional stone hearth oven built in New York. Our pasta menu blends a mix of traditional Italian recipes and our original creations. We have a seasonal menu which allows us to utilize fresh produce in its peak season such as asparagus, Walla Walla onions, fresh Washington apples and wild mushrooms.

One of our proudest accomplishments at Frankie's is our wine list. One of our goals is to have the best value wine list of any restaurant in the Seattle area. That means high quality wines at prices which are affordable. About two-thirds of our list is Italian. We also have a great selection of northwest wines.

Finally, I'd be remiss if I did not credit our staff for a big part of our success. These accomplishments would not exist without them. We've been blessed with many long term employees. Their loyalty and commitment have made our job so much easier and enriched the experience of those of you who are our customers. I'm proud to have them as part of our extended family. To them I say a hearty "mille grazie"!

Frankie's Pizza & Pasta, 16630 Redmond Way, Redmond, WA 98052 (425) 883 8407
www.frankiesredmond.com

About Frankie and family:

On a sunny June day in 1972, just after graduating from High School, grace and good fortune smiled upon me. I had just gotten promoted to assistant manager in my local McDonald's in Huntington Beach, when a cute little blond by the name of Rhonda walked in looking for a job. She got hired and a week later I asked her out on a date (fraternizing with the help -- a very big no-no!). She agreed, and the rest as they say, is history. I was a bit of a long-haired, wanna-be hippy (who wore a short-haired wig to work) and Rhonda was a little beach bunny. I fell head over heels, and that December we got married at the fully mature age of 19.

The two of us attended Orange Coast College in Costa Mesa, where I majored in photography; before getting swept up in my McDonald's career, and Rhonda and I starting a young family. For a time I managed the McDonald's franchise in HB and then one on Coast Highway in Newport Beach.

But Rhonda and I got a bug to escape the rat race of Orange County. In 1979 we visited friends in the quiet country suburb of Woodinville, Washington. We liked it so much we packed up our Volkswagen bus with our two kids and all our earthly possessions, and headed north on a grand adventure. We bought a house in Woodinville where we lived for 23 years and added two more children to our famiglia.

Rhonda did a long stint as a full-time mom, while I went off to continue my McDonald's career, working directly for the corporation this time around. The career went well. I eventually moved into mid-management. I did a variety of positions including supervising restaurants, being a Field Consultant to franchisees, and a Training Consultant teaching classes to managers.

McDonald's was a good job and an excellent teacher, but I never considered myself a corporate guy. I had a creative, entrepreneurial spirit and a yearning to launch out on my own. So for several years I honed my concept and, in 1993, Rhonda and I took a big leap of faith and opened Frankie's.

Neither Rhonda nor I have much formal training as chefs. But we both love to cook. So for many years I have applied myself to learning the craft of Italian cuisine. I attended continuing education classes at the Culinary Institute of America in Napa with my son Noah. And Rhonda and I have made two trips to Italy, immersing ourselves in the culture and food. But mostly, I have spent long hours in the kitchen, learning how to prepare traditional Italian dishes as well as creating my own original dishes from scratch. The best part has been enjoying the fruits of our labor.

Today our family includes a wonderful granddaughter, Teddy, who is the joy of our lives and my frequent helper in the kitchen. We have been blessed!

How Italians Eat

One of the things that I love about Italy is that the Italians eat their own cuisine almost exclusively. In the major cities like Rome, you may see an occasional Irish pub or Chinese restaurant. But these are frequented more by the tourists than the locals.

Dining habits of the Italian people are much different than that of Americans. Breakfast in Italy is not a significant event.. some toast, a pastry, croissant, or biscotti and of course some espresso. For many, their mid-day meal is the biggest of the day. In the small villages of the countryside, most of the town shuts down around 11:00 am and re-opens at 2:00, allowing for a leisurely lunch and perhaps a nap. Dinner, which is usually taken quite late (most restaurants don't even open until 8:00 or 9:00), is usually a lighter meal. It may be several courses but the quantities are not huge.

Wine is consumed with both lunch and dinner. It is not common to eat dessert after dinner. Some fruit would be more typical, possibly with cheese, followed by some sweet Moscato wine with a small biscotti, or some of that firewater they call grappa.

Sweets such as a pastry or gelato, would more likely be eaten as an afternoon snack.

Don't eat so fast!

You've all heard the saying "la dolce vita", "the sweet life". And you may have heard another... "la dolce far niente", "the sweetness of doing nothing". Neither they nor I are suggesting a life of idleness. But when you are through with a day's work, and sit down to eat and drink with your family, your friends, or maybe even by yourself; take a deep breath, take a sip of wine, and slow down. Raise your glass in a toast. Savor the food... every bite. Taste each morsel. Enjoy who you are with (even if just yourself). Breathe, exhale, and be thankful for these gifts.

If you've had the good fortune to visit Italy, and dine in their restaurants; you'll have noticed that the servers do not hover, they do not rush you. We American's sometimes misunderstand this as poor service. Not so. It is deeply rooted as part of their culture. They assume you will be there for hours, and that you wish to leisurely enjoy your food and those you are with.

The Italians believe that a meal, lovingly prepared is an integral part of 'la dolce vita". They even invented a movement, the "Slow Food" movement. It happened in reaction to a McDonald's opening near their sacred Spanish Steps. The idea of fast food made some of them *pazzo* (crazy) and began a revolution of sorts. The mission of those who began the this movement was to promote regional foods and wines, grown locally, and prepared using traditional methods.

Some believe the Slow Food movement has become too political. Yet their founding principles, and even their name, speak of a philosophy which I embrace with enthusiasm. Buon appetito!

Italian Cooking Philosophy

It is all about the ingredients!

That in a nutshell is what Italian cooking is all about. Though Italian cooking styles vary – by degree from village to village – and dramatically from north to south, it all has that one thing in common.

While the French pride themselves in their complex cooking methods, the Italians equally pride themselves in keeping it simple. Their goal is to place the fresh, flavorful ingredients front and center.

The Italians were cooking regionally and seasonally long before those concepts became the latest culinary fad to crash upon our shores (not that I oppose those ideas, I am ecstatic that we are finally grasping these ideals). An Italian cook first sees what is fresh in their garden, or their neighbor's garden, or the local weekly market – and then they plan their menu around that.

There are more reasons to eat locally grown, seasonal foods:

♦ Freshness of course being the most obvious. Foods grown close to home can be picked closer to their peak of ripeness.

♦ Which means the food tastes better. It is fresher and local growers are able to grow varieties of fruits and vegetables which are less commercially viable. Go to your local farmer's market and you will see colors and shapes never seen in the grocery store.

♦ It is better for the environment since food is not being shipped long distances.

♦ It helps support small family farmers as opposed to huge agricultural conglomerates.

♦ And more often than not these small farms are using organic growing methods, or at least avoiding the use of chemicals fertilizers and pesticides.

What is "Mis en place"?

Have you ever heard the term "mis en place"? If not, it is a term I would strongly encourage you to become familiar with, at least in concept!

Mis en place (pronounced MEEZ ahn plahs), is a French term which literally means "set in place".

This refers to arranging all of your recipe ingredients before you start cooking. All ingredients should be measured and ready to add to a dish, which includes all preparation such as chopping, dicing, grating, etc.

Mise en place makes the actual process of cooking easier and more efficient, and helps prevent you from making mistakes or discovering missing ingredients at the last moment. This will make you a better cook and far more relaxed in the kitchen.

My Italian Garden

Growing your own food can be fun and rewarding. And is the best is the best way to maximize freshness. Even if all you have is a small herb garden.

Have you ever bought fresh herbs at the grocery store? I once had to mortgage my house so I could buy herbs to make pasta! Even my cousin Vinnie in the old country grows a garden.

Anybody can have a garden. You don't need a lot of space. My son Chris and his wife Sandra live in a town home. They have no ground plot available so they keep a large pot of mixed herbs on their patio. My wife Rhonda and I have a home on a small lot so I have a small garden area along the sunny south side of the house. In some places it is only a foot or two wide and yet I manage to cram a lot into it. The sheltered warmth of the sun helps create a warmer micro-climate which some years makes it possible to grow warm weather vegetables such as tomatoes, peppers and eggplant. Sometimes I get lucky and they actually ripen. I also have several whiskey barrels tucked among the landscaping where I grow fresh salad greens and herbs. This year I added a small raised bed (only about twenty square feet) in the front of our home. The neighbors have enjoyed watching this little plot and were amazed at how much I coaxed out of such a small area.

No time to garden you say? It is true that a large garden can take a lot of time. But a small herb garden takes little time or skill. Some herbs such as rosemary and thyme are as effortless as any shrub, and can be tucked attractively amongst your other landscaping or in a pot.

They'll handle most Pacific northwest winters and the good news is that the slugs don't even like them!

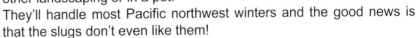

If you've got just a little more time and space, an herb garden is a good way to start. You can have a wonderful little herb garden with just 8 to 10 square feet of sunny ground; and if you locate it in a sunny spot near your kitchen you'll use it more.

It is a joy to watch stuff grow. With a little effort, you too can take part in the delicious richness of natures bounty.

Herbs I like to grow

A few tips for growing herbs:

Generally speaking, herbs prefer well drained soil and do not like added fertilizer. If growing in the ground, if your soil is dense and clay-like, add peat moss or similar soil amendments to lighten it up. If growing in pots, do not use potting soil with added fertilizers. These will just tend to make your herbs go to flower and seed quickly. Indoor potting soils which contain things like perlite (those little white pellets), work well.

A few herbs are easy to grow from seed, such as basil, parsley, thyme, chives and sage. Many others are difficult to do so, such as rosemary, oregano and tarragon. For these, it is much easier to buy starts.

Herbs for Italian cooking:

Fresh Basil: My favorite herb! It tastes like summer. Unless you plan to make pesto, one or two plants will be quite sufficient. Grow at least three or four if you want to make some fresh pesto from your garden (which freezes beautifully by the way).

Basil is an annual and loves warm weather. You can start it in May, but don't expect much from it until July. By the end of September, it will probably be history. That is unless you have planted it in a pot which you can bring indoors, extending its life for a couple of months.

Basil is an exception to the rule about herbs not liking to be fertilized. My local nurseryman taught me that basil especially flourishes with a little fish fertilizer. So I add that stinky stuff to my watering can every couple of weeks and water with it around the base of the plants. One thing to watch: the slugs like basil as much as you do!

Italian Parsley: I probably use more Italian Parsley than just about any other herb. It is great as both a flavor enhancer and as a garnish. It is easy to grow and handles cool weather much better than basil. It can also take a certain amount of shade. In mild winters it will go dormant without dying back completely. It is considered a biannual so it will sometimes last two years; but in my experience it will often flower and go to seed quickly in the second year. Therefore, I suggest planting some each spring.

Rosemary: A no brainer. It is easy to grow. The more mature the plant, the better its odds of surviving a harsh winter (it's a good idea to brush the snow off of them if you want to improve its odds). Rosemary is awesome in flavored olive oil, on focaccia bread, with roasted meats and in some sauces. It also makes a nice plant in your landscaping. Be aware however that their are trailing varieties available which are not good for culinary use.

Thyme: This herb is perfect for pots! It will creep a little if planted in the ground. If it is in a pot, make sure it is not under cover so it can get winter rain (unless you think you'll be disciplined enough to go out and water it in January). Thyme is great for soups and it is my favorite herb for flavoring olive oil!

Oregano: I consider this herb less essential than the previous three because, though easy to grow, it is a little bit of a troublemaker. It will take over your garden if planted in the ground. I grow mine in a whiskey barrel, but a large pot will also work well. Plant a few starts and forget about it. It will go dormant in the winter and proliferate 6 to 8 months out of the year. If you want to dry this herb, cut it as soon as it starts to get some flower buds. Tie it at the base of the stalks and hang it in a clean, cool, dry place. When it is dry, crush it between your hands and place in a spice jar or plastic zip lock bags.

Chives: Chives are a wonderful flavor enhancer or garnish. It is easy to grow in a pot but I find that it grows best in the ground; though it will die back in the winter. If grown in a pot, you can move it inside to a south or west windowsill in the fall. I cut mine back as soon as it begins to look scraggly in late fall. It will re-emerge green and vibrant in early spring.

Sage: Sage is great with white beans, soup, and of course, Thanksgiving stuffing. The plant is attractive and can last for many years. If it gets scraggly, just cut it back and it will come back healthier and bushier than ever. It will go dormant in the winter but will usually survive all but the most extreme winters.

Cilantro (aka Coriander): Hey, everybody gets in the mood for Mexican food once in a while. If you let it go after the leaves start to disappear you will eventually get little pods which are coriander seeds.

French Tarragon: French Tarragon is a little harder to grow, but it's well worth the trouble. You will likely have to purchase it as a plant, because it is hard to grow from seed. Like many herbs it will die back in winter and re-emerge in spring. It is less hardy than many herbs though, and there's a risk it may not survive a hard winter. I adore placing the leaves under the skin of a chicken before roasting. It's a perfect pairing with mushrooms. And it makes a nice alternative to traditional Italian herbs in tomato sauce.

Garlic: Need you ask why? Garlic not only tastes great but also has many health benefits. It strengthens your immune system and helps your body fight off infection.

Garlic bulbs grow from individual cloves which are planted in October for the following year's crop. It goes dormant in the winter and will come back to life as soon as the sun begins to warm the soil. It is ready to harvest in summer when the top part of the plants begins to turn brown and fall over. It needs little attention in between, other than periodic deep watering from mid-May until early July, while the bulbs are forming (depending on whether you have an early or late variety).

Buon appetito!

Some essential Ingredients

We on the west coast are blessed, in that we have a great variety and abundance of fresh local ingredients. And we also have excellent access to many products produced in Italy or made in the Italian style. Not everyone is so fortunate. My niece in Kentucky, who has tested several recipes for me, has had the greatest difficulty in locating ingredients such as ladyfingers or Mascarpone cheese; things we can find readily in our marketplace.

There are some ingredients which I feel you just cannot do without. Let's take a look...

Pasta: What is more fun than pasta? With all its fabulous shapes and sizes, it is a testament to the artistic genius of the Italian people! It's no wonder the Renaissance found it's roots in Italy.

Revisionist food historians now doubt the old myth that Marco Polo discovered noodles in China and brought them back to his Italian homeland. For the Greeks, located just across the sea, were making noodles long before Marco Polo emerged from his mother's womb.

In it's simplest form, pasta (literally "paste") is nothing more than flour, mixed with water, eggs, or both. Nearly eight centuries ago it was discovered that by drying it-- they could achieve a long shelf life, which meant it could be shipped all over Italy and eventually the world.

Fresh pasta vs dried: Many so-called "fresh" pastas are really dried. You will only find truly fresh pastas in the refrigerated section (this is necessary to keep them from going bad because of the moisture in them). I love the texture of fresh pasta but, unless I'm going to make it myself, I would just as soon stick with a good quality dried pasta.

And yet not all dried pasta is created equal. Poorly made pasta gives off excessive starch and tends to be mushy. It has been my experience that the Italians know how to make pasta better than most.

Two brands which I personally trust a lot are Barilla and De Cecco.

What are San Marzano Tomatoes?

You hear a lot about San Marzano tomatoes. True San Marzano tomatoes are a plum-type tomato grown in an area of Italy near Mount Vesuvius, close to Napoli. The soil there is very volcanic, giving the tomatoes their characteristic ashy flavor profile. Some chefs feel they are the best tomatoes in the world, especially for pizza and pasta sauces.

There are some brands from Italy which call themselves San Marzanos but are not the real thing. Genuine San Marzano's will show a DOP on the label, designating it as coming from within the boundaries assigned by the Italian government. There is also a domestic brand (which we happened to choose as one of our favorites), that uses the name San Marzano, but are actually grown and packed in California. Generally these non-official San Marzanos come from the same type of tomato plant as the genuine article.

So how did the true San Marzano's stack up in our taste test? Well we were only able to find one brand with the DOP designation. It ranked 13th out of 16 because we found them to be very bland. I am sure there are better brands out there. If you find them, please send them our way!

Tomatoes: Tomatoes are one of those rare exceptions where a "canned" product can be preferable to fresh. Not that you cannot make a good sauce from fresh tomatoes. Each year, if I am lucky enough to harvest enough fresh tomatoes from my garden, I make a batch of fresh tomato sauce. It's time consuming, but a labor of love. Yet most of the year (unless you live someplace like SoCal), you cannot get high quality fresh tomatoes. Those flavorless tomatoes you find in the grocery store are shipped from who-knows-where, or grown in a hot house. This is where high quality canned tomatoes come in. And the quality that you will find on your grocery store shelves can vary dramatically.

At Frankie's we use superb tomatoes which are packed immediately after harvest, at their peak of ripeness. Unfortunately they are not available to the consumer. Yet knowing the success of my recipes depended largely on the quality of tomatoes which go into them, I shopped the shelves of our local markets and selected 16 brands of Crushed Tomatoes for testing. The results are listed below.

Canned Tomato Tasting Results:

Knowing the success of my recipes largely depended on the quality of tomatoes which go in them, I shopped our local grocery stores and selected 16 brands of Crushed Tomatoes for testing. Our tasting panel was small, myself and my executive chef. But we were in total agreement on our favorites.

Our favorite Italian brand tomatoes:

Nina "Ground Pear Peeled" Tomatoes

These Nina brand tomatoes are a product of Italy. They were rich and very flavorful. And though not listed as San Marzano DOP Tomatoes, they had a slightly ashy, volcanic flavor which is characteristic of San Marzanos. Overall these were our favorite tomatoes we tasted.

Our favorite Domestic brand tomatoes:

San Marzano "Crushed" Tomatoes

Though these tomatoes have the name San Marzano, they are actually from California. Yet we found them superior to the San Marzano DOP tomatoes we were able to purchase locally. They have a bright tomato flavor and well balanced acidity. We liked them nearly as well as the Nina brand and they were much more widely available in our area.

Other brands we like include: Hunts "Organic Crushed" Tomatoes, Haggen "Italian-style Crushed" Tomatoes, Cento "All Purpose Crushed" Tomatoes (unsalted), Muir Glen "Organic— Ground Peeled" Tomatoes and DiNapoli "Crushed Tomatoes in Heavy Puree"

More essential Ingredients

In the pizza section of this book I provide a great deal of information about various cheeses. There is one though that I feel I should give special credence to and that is...

Parmigiano Reggiano: This cheese ranks among the great cheeses of the world. It is the ultimate table cheese, used throughout Italy. If you've never had a true Parmigiano-Reggiano, you don't know what "Parmesan" cheese is really supposed to taste like. And though it is relatively expensive (for home, we buy wedges at Costco), a little bit goes a long way.

Named for the cities of Parma and Reggio nell'Emilia, it can only be made in a precise agricultural zone covering portions of five Italian provinces, four in Emilia-Romagna and one in neighboring Lombardy; on the hills and plains enclosed by the rivers Po and Reno.

Parmigiano-Reggiano is a cow's milk cheese with a history that spans over nine centuries. Its production is tightly regulated. Fortunately, all wheels are stamped around their entire circumference so that it can always be identified as the genuine article.

Though no cheese can truly match Parmigiano-Reggiano's quality, there is a cheese made in other parts of Italy, known as Grana which bears some similarity. The best of these is Grana Padano. If you have limited resources, this is a better alternative than American-made Parmesan.

Cured Italian Meats:

What would Italian food be without cured Italian meats?

Prosciutto: The name derives from the Italian word "to dry" and literally means ham of any kind. The most famous of course is Prosciutto di Parma though there are many other excellent versions as well. At its best, prosciutto is rosy hued, silky in texture, with a slightly spicy aroma and a lightly salty, sweet-earthy flavor.

Pancetta: Italian Pancetta bears some similarity to our American bacon, but is typically not smoked like bacon. It is a dried, cured meat made from pork belly that has been cured with salt and spices, such as nutmeg, pepper, fennel, crushed red chiles and garlic.

Salami: The term Salami is very generic and covers dozens of varieties. Salami is basically a cured sausage, fermented and air-dried meat, originating from one of a variety of animals. Historically, salami has been popular among Southern European peasants because it can be stored at room temperature for periods. What we typically see called salami on menus is a Genoa-style salami. Some of my other favorites include Sopressata which is made in Calabria, and of course pepperoni!

Verdura (vegetables):

My favorite way to cook is to go out to the garden and pick something to make for dinner; possibly an eggplant fresh from the vine, or some tomatoes to make bruschetta with. It just does not get any fresher or healthier than that. As mentioned before, I do not have a large, sunny area to grow a garden, so I make do with a narrow garden bed down the south side of my

"My favorite way to cook is to go out to the garden and pick something to make for dinner; possibly an eggplant fresh from the vine, or some tomatoes to make bruschetta with."

house, and a small raised bed and some whiskey barrels tucked among my landscaping. I'm always surprised how much I can get from such a small area.

When you travel in Italy you see gardens everywhere; the back yard, on a roof top, or a precipitous hillside. The Italians know that growing your own vegetables is the best way to eat well.

But what if you don't have the time or space to grow your own vegetable garden? In my opinion, the next best option to growing your own vegetables is to buy directly from the farmer. This can be accomplished by going to farms which sell direct, or by going to your local farmer's market.

In Redmond where I live, we have a wonderful Farmer's Market, open every Saturday from April to October. Going there is one of my favorite things to do!

Olive Oil:

Olive oil is one of the true gifts from heaven! It tastes wonderful and has many health benefits. Does it get any better than that?

Pure Olive Oil: Pure olive oil is more refined than Extra Virgin, and thus not as tasty or good for you. Yet it does have its place. It has a higher smoke point and does not break down as readily when heated, making it a good choice for frying and sautéing.

Extra Virgin: I highly recommend Extra Virgin oils, which are made from first pressed olives, for dressings and any dish in which you want to get the full-flavor of the oil. Many people swear by Tuscan oils, but my friends who lived in Umbria for a year helped me to become a huge fan of Umbrian oils - though they can be hard to find.

Always look for the freshest oils you can find and store them in a cool, dark place.

$\mathcal{H}$ow we paired the food and wine

One of the best attributes of this book is that we've done the hard work (if you can call it that), of selecting wines to pair with each of the pizzas and pastas in this book. The pairings are listed with the recipes, along with fun and interesting information about the wine. I have listed both the "type" of wine, and a specific producer whose wine we are fond of with the food. If you cannot find that producer's wine, choose a wine from the type of wine listed.

I had the following criteria for the wines we selected....

First, I wanted only Italian wines. The first priority of Italian wine making is that the wine pairs well with food, because that is how they enjoy it. And whenever we could we paired regional foods with regional wines. Typically foods and wines that grow up together pair the best.

Secondly, I wanted affordable wines. All but a few of the wines fall into a $10 to $25 price range. This helps your pocketbook, and it is my experience that humble, casual food go better with these wines. The bigger, more expensive wines we tasted often overwhelmed the food. Save the expensive wines for your more upscale dinners with dishes like grilled beef or lamb.

Thirdly, I wanted the wines to be easy to find. This was the most challenging criteria since there are thousands of Italian wines available and most retailers carry a limited number of them. And I will say that we did list a few obscure wines here because they were clearly the best pairing. But be encouraged (especially if you live near our restaurant), because we can get any of these wines for you, and make them available to you at a good price.

Fourthly, the wine had to pair well with the food. This is critical of course. The wine should never overshadow the food. In a perfect pairing, the wine will invite you to take another bite of food, and a bite of the food will send you back for another sip of wine.

The Selection Process:

In the last year I conducted six tasting events, each with five or six of my wine reps and importers in attendance. They brought wines which they felt would pair well with a menu I had sent them in advance. We often tasted 25 to 30 wines. We would then bring out one dish at a time and taste the wines until we had some consensus on the best pairing (when we lacked consensus, guess who made the final choice?). We laughed a lot. And by the end we had purple teeth and were ready to be rolled out the door. It was great fun!

I would really like to say "mille grazie" to these wine reps for all their help. These people are pros. I could not have done it without them!

Italian wine 101

Italy is the largest vino producer in the world. And yet, they are not the world's largest exporter because they also consume more wine than probably any other country in the world. Most Italians drink wine with lunch, dinner and sometimes in between. To them, food and wine are inseparable.

I find that people are very interested in Italian wines, and yet, the number of wines is so vast and confusing that most people haven't a clue where to begin. So they buy the few wines they are familiar with (and that their local wine merchants carry: Chianti, Pinot Grigio, and maybe a Barbera or Montepulciano d'Abruzzo). There are entire books written on Italian wines, so I certainly am not going to teach you much here. But I would like to impart a few basics.

Firstly, like most Old World wines, Italian wines are more often named for the "place" they are grown than for the grapes which go into them. Thus the major source of confusion. That is because they believe that the "terrior", which is a combination of physical factors (soil, climate, elevation, sun exposure, etc.), are a bigger factor than the type of grape which goes into the wine. But they also have thousands of years experience in determining which grapes grow best in any given terrior.

Another big factor in Old World wines is that they do not (by law), irrigate their grape vines. They are at the mercy of Mother Nature. Thus, the vintage quality can vary more from year to year. It can be helpful to have a vintage chart when selecting Italian wines, or ask your wine merchant.

And by the way, we did not list vintages for the wines selected to pair with our recipes. I knew that such information would be outdated even before the book was published. And although there are differences in quality year-to-year, the basic essence of the wine will remain similar.

Italy has dozens of native grape varieties and over 350 authorized grape varieties and an additional 500 documented; many of which came to Italy from around Europe and the Mediterranean. From these they produce nearly a thousand different types of wines.

Today, Italy produces some of the finest wines in the world, and yet it was not always so. When Benito Mussolini was in power, he felt that wine should be cheaper than bread. With this philosophy, producers went for huge production but quality was not very good. In the last few decades however, there has been a major shift towards quality. It began in the north, and has gradually worked its way south. Today many of my favorite Italian wines come from the south. And they often come at bargain basement prices because they have yet to be discovered by the typical American consumer.

So where do we begin? As you peruse your way through the cook book, check out my wine pairing recommendations and read the notes. Doing so will give you some basis of knowledge. But hey, let's get real! The only way to really learn about the wines is to drink them. So break out of your rut. Search out some of these wines you've never tried before. And raise a glass to the ones you love!

Antipasti

Garlic Shrimp

We first developed this antipasti for our Garlic Festival several years ago. It was so popular that we had to put it on our menu or face riots from our customers.

Serves 6

1 loaf rustic Italian bread or French baguette

extra virgin olive oil (to brush on crostini)

2 teaspoons olive oil (for cooking)

20 medium sized shrimp --peeled and deveined

2 tablespoons chopped garlic

3/4 cup chopped tomatoes

2 teaspoons chopped Italian parsley

1/2 teaspoon garlic salt (or 1/4 teaspoon each of garlic powder & salt)

3 ounces dry white wine

juice of 1/2 medium-sized lemon

3 ounces butter—melted

1. Slice bread approximately 3/8 inch thick (If the bread has a large diameter, cut the slices in half). You will want 3-4 slices per person. Brush both sides with extra virgin olive oil.

2. Crostini may be toasted any number of ways; see note under Frankie's Tips below.

3. If shrimp are frozen, thaw under running cold water and pat dry with paper towels.

4. Heat olive oil over medium heat until oil just begins to shimmer.

5. Cook shrimp about half way (until they just begin to lose their translucence).

6. Add the garlic, tomatoes and parsley. Cook an additional 30-40 seconds.

7. Add wine, lemon juice and melted butter. Continue cooking briefly to incorporate flavors.

8. Transfer to an appropriate size rarebit, gratin pan or bowl and serve with warm crostini on the side (and lot's of napkins!).

Frankie's Tips:

♦ With a dish like this, your pre-preparation (mis-en-place--see page 10) is critical. Have all ingredients chopped and measured out because the shrimp will cook quickly and if you don't have all of the ingredients ready you can easily overcook the shrimp while doing so.

♦ Properly cooked shrimp are important to the success of this dish. Overcooked shrimp will shrink down too much and become dry and rubbery. Under cooked shrimp will still have some translucent flesh and taste fishy. Properly cooked shrimp will be white and coral-pink in color with no translucence remaining, and minimal shrinkage.

♦ Crostini may be prepared in advance if you like, and wrapped in foil and re-warmed in a low oven just before serving. There are any number of ways you can toast the Crostini... My favorite methods are grilling on a barbecue or using a Panini pan, because I like grill marks on my Crostini. You can also toast them under a broiler, in a toaster oven, or on a Panini grill (which will cook both side simultaneously), Otherwise, you will need to turn them over after the first side is properly toasted.

Grilled Sea Scallops wrapped in Pancetta

This is one of the easiest things you could ever prepare, and yet so delicious! For optimal success however, I would suggest using a piastra, which is a granite stone grill that you place atop your barbecue grate. They cost about $50 but are worth the investment for outdoor cooking. If you do not have one you could grill these atop foil, or even indoors in a cast iron skillet.

6 servings

1 pound (minimum one dozen) large sea scallops

6 ounces pancetta--sliced thickness of standard bacon

1/4 cup extra virgin olive oil

1/4 cup white wine

juice of one-half lemon

2 teaspoons fresh thyme (or fresh herb of your choice)—chopped

salt (preferably sea salt)

fresh ground black pepper

1. Put on some Italian music (Il Postino would be lovely!), and pour a glass of Italian white wine (you need some for the recipe anyway!).

2. In a shallow dish, blend together olive oil, wine and lemon juice. Add half of the herbs.

3. Dry scallops with paper towels. Wrap scallops with pancetta and place a toothpick through each to hold in place. Place wrapped scallops in a dish to marinate. Place in refrigerator for 30 minutes. Turn over and allow to marinate an additional 15 to 30 minutes.

4. If using a piastra (see note in introduction above), light your barbecue at least 20 minutes before grilling so the piastra has time to get nice and hot. You want a medium-high temperature.

5. Place scallops atop piastra (or foil) and season with salt and fresh ground pepper.

6. Grill until scallops brown nicely and begin to lose translucence. Gently turn over using tongs. Cook just until opaque.

7. Platter and sprinkle with remaining herbs.

Frankie's Tips:

♦ You really want to use sea scallops for this as opposed to bay scallops which are smaller and have a tougher texture. Also, fresh scallops are better than frozen, which tend to be more rubbery when cooked.

♦ Usually, the larger the scallops, the more expensive they are. You certainly don't need huge ones but medium-to-large ones are going to be easier to work with and make a nicer presentation. I would figure two to three per person depending on the size.

♦ Feel free to substitute a good quality bacon for the pancetta if you cannot find it. Prosciutto is also excellent, though not as juicy.

Monterosso, Cinque Terre

Positano on the Amalfi Coast

Bruschetta Pomodoro

In the dog days of summer, when tomatoes are hanging fat on the vine, I get a yearning this. This dish is best with fresh, high quality tomatoes! I don't like to use canned "diced" tomatoes because they are packed with chemicals to help them maintain their shape.

4 servings

1 pound fresh tomatoes

2 tablespoons fresh basil—julienned or torn in small pieces

1/4 teaspoon salt (preferably sea salt—coarse salt is also a nice option)

1-2 cloves fresh garlic—crushed

3 tablespoons extra virgin olive oil

more extra virgin olive oil for brushing on bread

1 loaf rustic Italian bread or French baguette

Parmigiano-Reggiano—shaved into small curls with vegetable peeler

1. Dice the tomatoes into 1/4 to 1/2 pieces. Place in a colander to drain excess juices.

2. Combine first five ingredients. Taste, and adjust salt to your liking. Leave out at room temperature to marinate.

3. Turn on barbecue (or start coals) and heat to medium.

4. Slice bread approximately 3/8 inch thick (If the bread has a large diameter, cut the slices in half). You will want 3-4 slices per person. Brush both sides with good quality olive oil.

5. Grill the bread until toasty and slightly crunchy with nice grill marks.

6. Platter and top with tomato mixture and garnish with Parmigiano.

Frankie's Tips:

♦ For optimum flavor and texture, do not refrigerate the tomatoes. Storage Tip: If you store tomatoes with the core side facing down, they will hold their freshness far longer than if stored with the core upward. You don't believe me? Test it out for yourself.

♦ This tomato topping is at its best if made one to three hours in advance so the flavors meld together.

♦ Capers are also a nice addition to this if you want to add a little more zip.

Crostini with Chicken Liver Spread

Cooks all over Tuscany and Umbria serve their own variation of this dish. Rhonda and I first had it at a wonderful little agriturismo in Umbria, where it was made as a smooth pâté. Recently we enjoyed it at an Antinori wine tasting at Chateau Ste. Michelle winery. This latter version had a coarser, more rustic texture, which we preferred. I will warn you that it is not the prettiest antipasti on the table, but you will think differently after you taste it!

Makes 24 Crostini— enough to serve 8-10

Crostini

24 slices rustic Italian bread—
(or 12 large, cut in half, yielding 24)

olive oil (for brushing on bread)

Chicken Liver Spread

8 tablespoons (1 stick) butter

2 medium shallots—diced small

8 small, fresh sage leaves—chopped

1 clove garlic

salt / ground black pepper

1 pound chicken livers—rinsed and patted dry—fat and connective issues removed

1/2 cup—dry white wine

2 tablespoons Capers—rinsed

1. Slice bread approximately 1/4 to 3/8 inch thick (if the bread has a large diameter, cut the slices in half). Brush both sides lightly with olive oil.

2. Crostini may be toasted any number of ways--see Frankie's Tips, page 22.

3. In a large sauté pan, heat the butter over medium-high heat until the foaming subsides. Add the shallot, sage, garlic and 1/4 teaspoon of salt (1/2 teaspoon if using unsalted butter). Cook, stirring regularly, until the shallot softens—3-4 minutes.

4. Add the chicken livers and toss, cooking briefly—about one minute.

5. Add wine and scrape bottom of the pan to get up all the flavorful bits. Reduce heat and simmer 4 to 5 minutes until the wine is cooked down and becomes syrupy. The chicken livers should still have a rosy interior.

6. Transfer all of the pan contents to a food processor fitted with a steel blade. Process, using short one second pulses until coarsely chopped (about 6-8 pulses). Transfer to a clean bowl.

7. Stir in capers, and adjust salt and pepper to taste.

8. While still warm, spread spoonful on each crostini and serve immediately. Garnish with additional sprigs of sage on the platter or a small leaf atop each crostini.

Frankie's Tips:

♦ One ingredient which Italians often add to this is anchovies. I prefer it without, but if you like anchovies, feel free to add one or two at the same time you add the chicken livers.

♦ Two keys to the success of this dish is to use fresh, plump Chicken Livers; and to trim them well. Old liver will taste metallic, and untrimmed liver will be stringy and fibrous.

♦ It is also important not to overcook the livers. Liver which is over-cooked will produce a spread which is dry, mealy, and bland in flavor.

♦ The spread can be made up to a day ahead and refrigerated. Warm in a microwave or low oven before serving.

Caponata

With grilled eggplant and heirloom tomatoes

Caponata is a sweet-and-sour eggplant relish from Sicily. It was only recently that I had the good sense to make some. We were to bring antipasti to some friends for dinner and I wanted to try something I had never made before. I researched many Caponata recipes, and found that they vary significantly beyond a few basic ingredients. Some show the North African influence which often displays itself in Sicilian cooking; with the addition of ingredients such as cinnamon, cocoa, and raisins or dried currants. We arrived at our friends and amazingly they had just such a version in their refrigerator which they'd made a few days earlier. It was a great comparison. They were very different but both superb.

Caponata can be eaten on plates with forks, or on top of crostini. It also makes an excellent relish for serving with meats: such as grilled pork roast or even fish.

Makes 6 cups - enough to feed 12

1 medium to large eggplant--cut into 3/4 inch cubes

1/2 cup extra virgin olive oil (plus extra for brushing crostini if making)

1 red bell pepper--stemmed, seeded and cut into 3/4 inch pieces (optional)

3 ribs of celery--cut into 3/4 inch lengths

1 medium onion--chopped

1/2 cup capers--rinsed

1/2 cup pitted green olives--rough chopped

1 pound fresh tomatoes (preferably heirlooms)--cut into 3/4 inch cubes

1 tablespoon minced fresh oregano

1/4 cup fresh basil--roughly chopped

1/4 cup red wine vinegar

1 tablespoon sugar

salt (to taste)

1 loaf crusty Italian bread (optional for crostini)

1. Heat a vegetable grill pan or piastra (see intro on page 24), on a barbecue. Toss eggplant cubes with half of the oil. Grill until nicely browned and tender. Place in a large bowl to cool.

2. In a cast iron skillet or large sauté pan, heat the remaining 1/4 cup oil over medium-high heat. Add the red pepper and stir and cook for about a minute. Add celery and onion and continue cooking until all vegetables are slightly browned and softened. Remove from pan and set aside to cool.

3. After all vegetables have cooled to room temperature, mix with remaining ingredients. Taste and add salt if you desire. Refrigerate for up to 3 days.

4. If you plan to serve with crostini, slice bread approximately 1/4 to 3/8 inch thick. Brush both sides lightly with olive oil.

5. Crostini may be toasted any number of ways--see Frankie's Tips, page 22.

Frankie's Tips:

♦ This recipe is very flexible! Add or deduct ingredients, or change quantities to your hearts content. Some other common ingredients include anchovies (just 1 or 2 fillets) and raisins. You can also substitute different type of olives, or use white wine vinegar.

♦ Feel free to sauté eggplant as opposed to grilling it. I chose grilling to impart a slightly smoky character.

♦ Any kind of tomatoes will work. Many recipes call for canned diced tomatoes, or crushed or even tomato sauce. Heirlooms have such awesome flavor I decided to use those.

Stuffed Cremini Mushrooms

This filling recipe is essentially the same as we've been featuring on our Frankie's catering menu for years (other than a couple of small improvements made during re-testing). We use regular button mushrooms--since we always have them on hand. But I wanted to upscale it a little for the book so I used large Cremini mushrooms. You could also use Portobello mushrooms. If doing so, I would consider the Baby Portobellos if you can find them, as a large Portobello makes for a pretty large serving.

16 ~ 18 large Cremini Mushrooms enough to serve 8 to 10

18 large Cremini mushrooms

Stuffing:

4 ounces pancetta--diced small

1 tablespoon olive oil

1/4 cup onion—finely minced

1/4 cup red bell pepper—finely minced

1/3 teaspoon salt (preferably sea salt)

3 ounces cream cheese--at room temperature

1/4 teaspoon Worcestershire sauce

Bread Crumb Topping:

1 tablespoon butter--melted

1/2 cup homemade bread crumbs (see notes below)

1 tablespoon fresh tarragon or Italian parsley—chopped (I prefer tarragon)

1. Wash and dry mushrooms. Remove stems and chop into small pieces. Place stems in a mixing bowl. Place mushroom caps on a baking sheet.
2. Heat olive oil over medium heat in a large sauté pan. Cook pancetta until slightly crispy. Transfer to a paper towel. Leave fat and juices in skillet.
3. Add onions and red bell peppers to skillet. Cook over low-medium heat until softened. Place in mixing bowl with chopped mushroom stems to cool.
4. Place butter in the sauté pan and melt over low heat. Turn off heat and add bread crumbs and tarragon (or parsley). Toss well and set aside.
5. Preheat oven to 400 F.
6. To the bowl with the mushroom stems, onions and peppers; add salt, cream cheese, Worcestershire, and pancetta. Mix well. Fill mushrooms with mixture.
7. Sprinkle bread crumb mixture on top of filling.
8. Bake 20 minutes until bread crumbs are nicely browned.

Frankie's Tips:

♦ The number of mushrooms you can fill with this stuffing can vary a lot depending on the size of the mushrooms. With small mushrooms you could get as many as 30 to 35. With large Portobellos, it could be as few as 5 to 6.

Making homemade bread crumbs from scratch:

Homemade bread crumbs are best made from old, stale bread. Fresh bread will not process well. Yet, I rarely have stale bread. To solve this problem, you can set it out overnight, or place bread in a 200° F oven for 3-5 minutes to dry it out. Once dry, remove crusts. Then process in a food processor, using short 2-3 second bursts, until the bread crumbs are coarsely chopped (you want them to be a bit coarser than store bought bread crumbs).

Foccacia e Foccacia Verde

Foccacia bread is very easy to make. You can make your own pizza dough. Or you can pick up some dough from your favorite pizzeria (like Frankie's), or purchase bread dough from the grocery store. Vary the thickness to your liking. If you don't have a pizza stone, bake on an oiled aluminum pan at 450 F.

The Foccacia Verde is a simple variation with fresh basil pesto sauce and four cheeses. So yummy!

6 servings

Foccacia Bread:

1 medium pizza dough (or bread dough)

2 tablespoons extra virgin olive oil

1-2 cloves garlic—pressed or minced

salt (I like a little coarse sea salt)

fresh herbs--such as rosemary, tarragon or thyme (or combination of)

1 tablespoons fresh basil leaves (small leaves or larger leaves torn)

Foccacia Verde:

instead of olive oil, garlic, salt and herbs, top the dough with...

1 to 2 tablespoons fresh basil pesto

Quattro Formaggio cheese blend (see Quattro Formaggio pizza, page 83, or create your own blend)--light quantity

Foccacia Bread:

1. Place pizza stone in oven and set temperature to 475 F. Pre-heat at least 45 minutes prior to use.

2. If pizza dough is cold, set out at room temperature for 20 to 30 minutes prior to using. Flour work surface. Roll out the pizza dough to a 10-12 inch circle. Then, using your fingertips, create indents in the dough. Transfer dough to well floured wooden pizza peel.

3. Top the focaccia with olive oil, garlic, a light amount of salt and some herbs. Use wood peel to transfer onto the hot pizza stone.

4. Bake 7 to 9 minutes, or until the edges are light brown and firm to the touch.

5. Cut into wedges. Top with fresh basil.

Foccacia Verde:

1. Brush fresh basil pesto on dough or drizzle randomly for a more rustic look.

2. Use a light quantity of cheese and spread it to the edges (see Frankie's Tip's on next page).

3. Bake as you would a standard Foccacia.

Foccacia Pomodoro

This version of Focaccia uses a topping of tomatoes, olive oil, garlic and basil, not unlike the Tomato-Basil relish I make for Bruschetta. The difference here is the addition of balsamic vinegar and capers. The balsamic gives a touch of sweet and sour while the capers add a salty spiciness. Buon appetito!

6 servings

1 medium pizza dough (or bread dough)

1-1/2 cup chopped fresh tomatoes—juices drained

2 tablespoons extra virgin olive oil

1 teaspoon balsamic vinegar

2 tablespoons capers—rinsed and drained

1-2 cloves garlic—pressed or minced

1 tablespoons fresh basil leaves (small leaves or larger leaves torn)

Parmigiano-Reggiano—shaved into small curls with vegetable peeler

1. Place pizza stone in oven and set temperature to 475 F. Pre-heat at least 45 minutes prior to use.

2. Chop tomatoes. Place in a colander or mesh strainer, and allow to sit for several minutes to allow juices to drain. Place in a bowl and mix in olive oil, balsamic, capers and garlic.

3. If pizza dough is cold, set out at room temperature for 20 to 30 minutes prior to using. Flour work surface. Roll out the pizza dough to a 10-12 inch circle. Then, using your fingertips, create indents in the dough. Transfer dough to well floured wooden pizza peel.

4. Top the focaccia with the tomato mixture (see Frankie's Tip's below). Give the pizza peel a shake to ensure the focaccia is not sticking to the peel. Then use the pizza peel to transfer the focaccia onto the hot pizza stone.

5. Bake 7 to 9 minutes, or until the edges are light brown and firm to the touch.

6. Cut into wedges. Top with basil and shavings of Parmigiano-Reggiano.

Frankie's Tips:

♦ One little thing... on a Foccacia which has toppings such as the Foccacia Verde or Pomodoro, if you don't put the toppings all the way out to the edge of the dough, the dough will puff up where it is not covered. This will make your Foccacia look more like a pizza than a flat bread, which it is intended to be.

Pizzette

Here's something fun for a party... little pizzas with a variety of toppings. You can make them ahead and serve them at room temperature, or re-warm before serving. Or set up a pizza bar and let each guest create their own. Don't worry about having them round. Just stretch the dough into random shapes for a more rustic look. You can make your own pizza dough or buy some pre-made bread or pizza dough.

Below I've listed some favorite toppings that I did not list in the pizza section of this book.

6 servings as a main course
12 as an appetizer

one batch of pizza dough (or 2-3 store-bought bread doughs)

pizza sauce

basil pesto sauce (optional)

cheeses of your choice

all purpose flour (for dusting counter)

corn meal or flour (to dust pizza peel)

assorted toppings

1. Put on some Italian music and pour a glass of wine.

2. If making your own dough, it is best to make it in the morning or the day before. See Pizza Dough recipe in the Pizza chapter of this book.

3. Prepare pizza sauce (or use store bought if you want to keep it simple). Same with Basil Pesto sauce.

4. Place pizza stone in oven and set temperature to 500 F. Pre-heat at least 45 minutes prior to use (or bake on an aluminum sheet pan at 450 F).

5. Prep toppings. Grate cheeses if whole block.

6. On a lightly floured counter, divide dough into a dozen or more pieces of roughly 3 ounces each and stretch to roughly a 4 inch diameter.

7. Place corn meal or flour on pizza peel (so dough does not stick). Place about 4 doughs on the peel at a time. Top with sauce, cheese and ingredients of your choice.

8. Transfer to pizza stone, trying not to allow them to touch (if they do, move them with a long spatula after they have baked for one minute).

9. Bake until the crust is brown and firm on the edges, and your cheese is fully melted and beginning to brown (6 to 8 minutes). Use pizza peel or long spatula to remove.

Some of my favorite combinations:

♦ Mozzarella and Feta cheeses with tomatoes and fresh basil

♦ Basil pesto with goat cheese, red onions & artichoke hearts

♦ Sausage-garlic (or roasted garlic)

♦ Sausage & gorgonzola cheese

♦ Fresh mozzarella with sausage & sun-dried tomatoes

♦ Salami and provolone cheese with mixed olives

♦ Sweet sausage & provolone

♦ Pepperoni & red cherry peppers

Frankie's Tips:

♦ If you've never made pizza from scratch, may I suggest you read the *Making Pizza at Home* section of the Pizza chapter, before you begin.

♦ If doing a large variety of Pizzette, keep in mind that you'll only use a small amount of each topping, so keep it simple, and purchase ingredients which you will use at other meals.

My heritage

By Frankie... excerpt from my book "A Full Moon Over Tuscany"

Almost daily I hear the question... "Are you Italian"? or "What part of Italy are you from"? Many want to know if I or my family come from Italy. Others just assume that I'm of Italian heritage.

The answer is not so simple. Let me explain by including the following excerpt from a book I wrote following our first trip to Italy...

I don't know why Italy has been such a magnet to me, but it seems as though for most of my life, the power of all things Italian has grown like a porcini mushroom in my life.

I've always loved the food, which might explain of course why I opened an Italian restaurant. This in turn led to a love of Italian wines. But that is only the beginning of this story.

By bloodline, I can find no record of Italian blood in my ancestry. But somehow, somewhere, a bit of it must have snuck in. For one thing, I look a little Italian. And who, other than someone of that ancestry would name their son Frank? Every other Frank I know or have even heard of is Italian. I rarely ever meet any other Frank's except for when I go to restaurant food shows and I hear their names announced over the loud speaker system, "Will Frank Carlucci please meet Frank Giovanni at the sausage booth".

I was named after my grandfather who had been adopted by the Curtiss family. I'm told that his blood name was Natur, which is Danish. But who among the Danes would name their son Frank as opposed to say Sven or Thor? One of my theories is that they were maybe running from the Mafia or something, and when they were found out, they adopted out their son for his protection. They would of course have made up a name like Natur that was so unusual as to be believed.

Some years ago (long before Frankie's), a co-worker of mine saw a photo of my extended family and asked if my family was Italian. Further evidence I believe of the truth of it all. I explained that we were mostly dark Danes (my mother was also mostly Danish) and that my half brother and sister also had olive complexion because their father was French.

But who are these "dark" Danes anyway and where did they come from? I thought Scandinavian people were fair skinned and blond? Could it be the influence of some Roman conquerors, or some who migrated north to escape their tyranny?

Enough of this scandalous talk! I should accept who I am, a European "mutt" and be done with it! Yet owning an Italian restaurant has just brought forth a certain schizophrenia about it all. People either assume I'm Italian (see I told you I looked Italian) or want to believe I am. It lends more credibility. Not being Italian leaves me feeling insecure as a result. And never even having been to Italy; well that just made matters worse. So off we go.

Their next assumption (or hope), is that if I'm not Italian I must at least be from the Bronx. It could never be that a Danish boy from the west coast would know how to cook Italian! And yes, I believe that I do have a gift for making great Italian food. Why would God give such a talent to a Dane?

So there you go. A clear cut answer don't you think?! Gotta run now... I Need to call my cousin Giovanni.

Castelnuevo dell'Abate, near M

Zuppa, Insalata e Panini

Italian Wedding Soup

The origins of this soup, a variant of minestrone, are "soupy" shall we say. And nobody knows for sure exactly how or when it first became connected to weddings. Food historians believe the term "wedding soup" is a mis-translation of the Italian language, minestra maritata ("married soup"), which refers to the idea that green vegetables and meats in a clear broth go well together; forming the "perfect" marriage!

Its ingredients and style probably date back to the Romans, but its name is thought to be of more recent origin. Today, you'll find many Italian-American families who insist the soup is traditional at weddings. This may be how it managed to keep its name throughout the decades.

But surely this soup is too good to be served only at weddings! At Frankie's we originally made it just here-and-there as a soup-of-the-day, but the demand was so great we nearly had to call in the riot police. Now it has become our most popular soup.

Serves 8 as a first course

1 ounce olive oil

12 ounces spicy Italian sausage

2 tablespoons butter

1 cup onions--finely diced

1 cup carrots--finely diced

1/2 cup celery--finely diced

1/2 cup basil pesto (see Frankie's Tips)

3 cups fresh spinach--cleaned and chopped

1 quart chicken stock

1/4 lb. Acini di Pepe pasta (or Orzo)

grated Parmigiano-Reggiano cheese (optional for garnish)

1. Heat oil in a soup pot over medium heat. Add sausage. Chop thoroughly and stir with a wooden spatula until the pink is gone. Drain meat and set aside.

2. Return empty soup pot to stove. Melt butter over medium heat. Add onion, carrots, and celery and sauté until softened, about 4 to 5 minutes.

3. Add spinach and sauté until it just starts to wilt.

4. Stir in basil pesto. Add Chicken stock.

5. Add back the Italian sausage.

6. Reduce heat. Simmer 10 to 12 minutes, stirring periodically.

7. Add pasta and cook for an additional 6 to 8 minutes.

8. Top bowls with freshly grated Parmigiano-Reggiano.

Photos: Left to right from top

- Italian Wedding Soup
- Vegetable Minestrone
- Zuppa Bolognese with White Beans
- Tuscan White Bean Soup
- Lentil Soup with Sausage
- Creamy Roasted Red Pepper Soup
- Creamy Tomato-Gorgonzola Soup
- Fennel and Leek Soup

Frankie's Tips:

- You can use store bought pesto for this, but making your own is better. I have a recipe in the pasta section on page 110. Pesto freezes well. I usually make a double recipe once or twice each summer with basil I grow in my garden. I transfer the pesto to 4 oz. disposable food containers and pour a thin layer of olive oil over the top, which keeps it fresh and green (this can also be done with leftover pesto which you plan to store in the refrigerator).

- Acini di Pepe (pronounced *ah-CHEE-nee dee peh-pay*) is a very small pasta shaped like tiny beads. If you cannot find it you can substitute orzo or any other small pasta shape.

Vegetable Minestrone Soup

This is the recipe for Vegetable Minestrone which we have sold at Frankie's from day one. We tested some variations on it before putting it in the book and decided that it was best just the way it was.

Minestrone comes from the root word *minestra*, which simply means soup. Minestrone means "big soup" because it generally has a lot of ingredients in it. It's usually made with whatever vegetables are in season. Every Italian family has their own recipe, so don't hesitate to play around with it to your liking. Things like onions, leeks, swiss chard, and kale would all be wonderful additions. You can also use any types of beans you prefer.

And of course it doesn't have to be vegetarian. You can use chicken stock instead of vegetable stock and add meats such as sausage or pancetta if you like.

8 servings

1 tablespoon olive oil

1 stalk celery--diced small

1 medium carrot peeled--diced small

1 medium zucchini--diced small

2 teaspoons chopped garlic

1 tablespoon salt

1 teaspoon fresh ground black pepper

2 bay leaves

28 ounce can (or 2 - 15 ounce cans) diced tomatoes in juice

2 - 32 ounce containers vegetable stock

15 ounce can kidney beans--drained

15 ounce can garbanzo beans--drained

4 cups water

3 tablespoons fresh basil pesto (optional--see Frankie's Tip's)

1/4 pound penne pasta--pre-cooked

1. Heat olive oil in soup pot. Add all celery, carrots and zucchini. Sauté until they begin to soften.

2. Add garlic, salt, pepper and bay leaves. Stir and sauté well for about a minute to loosen the flavors.

3. Add the canned tomatoes, vegetable stock, kidney and garbanzo beans, water and basil pesto (optional).

4. Simmer for about a half hour.

5. Add pasta. Heat for a minute or two longer.

6. Remove bay leaves before serving. Doesn't some delicious Italian bread sound perfect with this?

Frankie's Tips:

♦ Like many soups, this one is better the second day, after the flavors have fully melded together.

♦ If you've made my basil pesto recipe (page 110), and placed some in 4 ounce containers as suggested, you'll have some in your freezer to add to the soup. It adds another dimension of flavor. You could also buy some at the market, but its expensive and not as good. Another alternative is to simply add some fresh basil with extra virgin olive oil and a bit of parmesan cheese.

♦ The reason we pre-cook the pasta instead of cooking it in the soup is to avoid excess starchiness.

♦ Also, save your rinds when you finish a chunk of Parmigiano-Reggiano (place in a storage bag in the freezer). Throw a rind in your soup while its cooking. Its a wonderful flavor enhancer!

Zuppa Bolognese with White Beans

This soup is something I came up with while playing around in the kitchen at Frankie's one day. It was a cold day out and I wanted something hearty and delicious, and this started coming together in my mind. It has many of the same ingredients as our Bolognese sauce, though I used Italian sausage instead of ground beef. And of course white beans are never added to Bolognese sauce. Nonetheless, this soup turned out even better than I had hoped and is now one of my all time favorites!

8 servings

1 pound dried Great Northern white beans

2 ounce olive oil

8 ounces pancetta (or bacon)--diced

1-1/2 pounds spicy Italian sausage

2 cups chicken stock

24 ounces Marinara sauce

1 tablespoon dried basil

2 teaspoons dried oregano

1 cup onions--finely chopped

1 cup celery--finely chopped

1 cup carrots--finely chopped

3 to 4 cloves fresh garlic--minced

1-1/2 cups dry white wine

2 cups half & half

salt and pepper

1. Place beans in large soup pot with 6 cups of water and soak 8-10 hours (or see *Tips on Handling Dried Beans*, page 47, for quick soak method).

2. Pour beans into a colander to drain. Rinse and dry soup pot.

3. In a separate skillet, heat olive oil over medium heat. Cook pancetta and Italian sausage.

4. While meat is browning--place beans, chicken stock, marinara, and dried basil and oregano in soup pot and bring to a low boil.

5. When meat is browned, transfer to soup pot with a slotted spoon, leaving the fat in the skillet. Add celery, carrots and onions to skillet and cook until onions translucent. Add garlic and cook about one minute.

6. Add white wine to skillet. Stir and simmer until wine has reduced by about a third (this step is known as deglazing). Add to soup pot and continue simmering until beans are tender--about 20 to 30 minutes.

7. Stir in half and half and serve.

Frankie's Tips:

♦ This soup is so good I hesitate to suggest any variations. I will mention though that you could use canned beans instead of dried. If you do so, place in a colander and rinse before adding.

♦ This recipe may make a larger quantity than you desire but the leftovers are even better than on the first day. And it will freeze well if you'd prefer not to eat it all within a few days.

Tuscan White Bean Soup
with Pancetta and fresh Sage

This soup is so delicious that I have customers who ask us to telephone them whenever we serve it. It is soul-warming, rustic peasant food, the type you'd be more likely to find in a casual trattoria than a Michelin rated ristorante.

6 servings

1 pound dried Great Northern white beans

2 tablespoon olive oil

1/2 cup red pepper—diced

3/4 cup onions—diced

2-3 cloves minced garlic

1/4 cup fresh sage—chopped

1/2 lb. pancetta—sliced thick (or un-smoked, thick-sliced bacon)

2 quarts chicken stock (preferably low-sodium)

1 teaspoon garlic salt (or 1/2 teaspoon garlic powder and increase salt)

1/2 teaspoon salt

1/4 teaspoon celery salt

black pepper—fresh ground

1 cup fresh grated Parmigiano-Reggiano

1. Place beans in large stock pot with 6 cups of water and soak (see Tips on Handling dried beans--next page).
2. Pour beans into a colander to drain. Dry stock pot.
3. Add 1 tablespoon olive oil to the stock pot and warm over medium heat until it just begins to shimmer. Add red peppers and onion and sauté 3-4 minutes. Add garlic and sage and continue to cook until onions are translucent—about 8-10 minutes.
4. While onions and peppers are cooking, cook pancetta in a separate skillet with 1 tablespoon of olive oil until barely crisp. Drain on paper towels. Chop and set aside.
5. When onions and peppers are cooked, add chicken stock and beans along with garlic salt, salt, celery salt and several turns of fresh ground black pepper. Add most of the Pancetta (reserve some for garnish).
6. Bring to a boil over medium-high heat, then reduce heat to a simmer and cook until beans are just tender—about two hours—adding water or additional stock as needed to keep beans barely covered. Turn off heat.
7. Remove approximately a quarter of the beans. Puree in food processor fitted with steel blade. Add back to soup. Taste and adjust seasoning to taste.
8. Place in bowls and garnish with Parmigiano-Reggiano and chopped Pancetta (and/or additional fresh sage).

Frankie's Tips:

♦ In this recipe, I've used a separate skillet to cook the Pancetta (or bacon), but if you want to make this a one-pot-meal, cut up the pancetta and cook it in the stock pot. Cook until it is just beginning to crisp, before adding the garlic and sage. The extra fat rendered adds even more flavor to the soup, but will result in bits of pork residue ending up in the finished soup.

♦ If you are not crazy about sage, try a different herb. A frequently used alternative in Tuscany is rosemary (a friend of ours used both sage and rosemary); but feel free to use any herb you want.

♦ Also feel the liberty to use fresh celery in the soup instead of celery salt. Dice the celery small and add along with the onions and red peppers.

♦ This soup is also wonderful with spinach or other greens which can be added when onions are almost done cooking. Sauté until wilted.

Tips on Handling Dried Beans:

I did some research and found the following information, posted by one of the bean companies, regarding proper handling of dried beans. I thought it was very useful so I included it here.

Storing Dried Beans: Dry beans should be stored at room temperature in covered containers. They will keep almost indefinitely. Do not keep dry beans in the refrigerator. If stored incorrectly, the beans may absorb water and spoil before you have a chance to use them.

The plastic bags beans are packaged in are good for storage if they are airtight. Once opened, the bag may be re-closed with a twist tie. For the longest storage life, keep beans in a glass or plastic container with a tight fitting lid.

Sorting Beans: Sorting means picking over the beans before cooking them. Remove small rocks, pieces of dirt, beans with holes or cavities, badly misshapen or wrinkled beans and those greatly undersized or discolored.

Soaking Beans: Soaking is not an essential step in bean preparation. The purpose of soaking is to begin rehydration before cooking, thereby reducing cooking time. Un-soaked beans take longer to cook and require more attention so they won't cook dry.

During soaking, beans make up their lost water, increasing up to twice their dried size. Enough water must be used to keep the beans covered while soaking. Once rehydrated, beans cook in 1 to 3 hours, depending on the type of bean.

There are basically two methods for soaking: long-soak and quick-soak. Both work equally well and differ only in the amount of time required to rehydrate the beans. Choose the one which best suits your time and schedule.

Long-soaking Method: Long-soaking takes time and some advance planning, but needs very little effort. First, cover the beans with water at room temperature. Soak them overnight or for 8 to 10 hours. Keep the beans covered by water while soaking. Be sure the soak water is at room temperature. Hot water may cause the beans to sour. Cold water slows rehydration and the beans will take longer to cook.

Cooking time will also be longer if beans are not soaked long enough (at least 8 hours). Beans soaked longer than 12 hours can absorb too much water and lose their characteristic texture and flavor. If you plan to cook beans for dinner and you want to use the long-soak method, start soaking first thing in the morning. To cook beans for lunch, you'll need to soak them overnight.

Quick-soaking Method: For most cooks, this is the most convenient method. Quick-soaking rehydrates dried beans in a little more than 1 hour—but four hours or more is even better as it will allow a greater amount of sugar to dissolve, thus helping the beans to be more easily digested.

Bring the beans and water for soaking to a boil. Boil for 2 minutes. Remove the beans from the heat and cover the pot. Let the beans stand in the soak water for 1 to 6 hours. At the end of that time, discard the soak water and cook the beans.

Lentil Soup with Sausage

In Italy there is a tradition that eating lentils on New Years Eve, symbolizes the desire to earn more money next year, most likely because of their round, coin-like shape. This is one of those soups I yearn for when the weather cools down. As I often quote to my granddaughter... "it's delicious and nutritious". Lentils are high in protein, fiber, iron, and essential amino acids. I like to make this with Chicken Italian Sausage which makes it even healthier, and just as tasty in my opinion.

6 servings

1 tablespoon cup olive oil

12 to 16 ounces bulk Italian sausage--
(sweet or hot / chicken or pork)

1 medium onion—diced

3-4 cloves garlic--minced

1 teaspoon ground turmeric

1 teaspoon ground cumin

1/2 teaspoon chili powder

1/2 teaspoon salt

fresh ground black pepper--to taste

28 oz. can crushed tomatoes

1 quart (32 ounces) chicken stock

2 to 3 cups water

1 pound dried lentils

2 to 3 tablespoons Italian parsley--
chopped

1. Rinse and sort Lentils per package directions.

2. Drizzle olive oil in a soup pot. Heat over medium-high heat until oil begins to shimmer. Add sausage. Chop and stir until most of the pink is gone. Drain excess fat. Add onions and garlic and continue to cook until onions are softened—about 4-5 minutes.

3. Add all spices. Stir and sauté briefly to incorporate and enhance flavors.

4. Add crushed tomatoes, chicken stock, 2 cups of water and lentils.

5. Bring to a boil over medium-high heat, then reduce heat to a simmer and cook for one hour—adding additional water if you feel the soup needs it.

6. If you have a rotary hand blender, use it to puree some of the soup for 5 to 10 seconds (or remove approximately a quarter of the soup and puree in food processor fitted with steel blade). Add back to soup.

7. Add Italian Parsley. Taste and adjust seasoning to your liking.

Frankie's Tips:

♦ Lentils are legumes that generally have a rich, nutty flavor. Dried lentils are very inexpensive, making this a great budget meal while your saving money for Christmas.

♦ Because of their small size, lentils cook much faster than beans and so do not require soaking.

♦ If the sausage you purchase comes in links, remove from casing prior to cooking. Pancetta is also excellent in this soup.

♦ It is not a necessity to puree some of the soup as shown in step 5. I just like the texture better.

Creamy Roasted Red Pepper Soup

This soup is rustic, and yet elegant at the same time. And the roasted red peppers give it a deep, rich flavor. If you've never roasted red peppers, you will be surprised how easy it is! As is, this is a vegetarian recipe. If you desire a heartier meal, you can add cooked meat to it such as diced chicken, sausage, pancetta (or bacon), or even smoked salmon.

6 servings

2 pounds (or more) red bell peppers

2 tablespoons olive oil

2 to 3 shallots--chopped

3 to 4 cloves fresh garlic--minced

4 large fresh basil leaves--julienne cut (consider additional for garnish)

2 teaspoons fresh thyme--chopped

1 teaspoon salt

1/2 teaspoon fresh ground black pepper

1 tablespoon white wine vinegar

2 cups vegetable stock

1 cup half and half

6 ounce can tomato paste

1/4 cup sour cream mixed with 2 tablespoons milk (optional for garnish)

1. Char or roast red peppers until the peppers are blackened on all sides (see Frankie's Tips). Sweat peppers by placing in a paper bag or large zip-lock bag until cool enough to handle. Peel peppers, cut off tops, remove seeds and cut into chunks.

2. Heat oil in soup pot over medium heat. Add diced shallot and sauté until tender, about 4 to 5 minutes. Add garlic and sauté for one minute.

3. Add basil, thyme, salt, pepper, roasted red peppers and white wine vinegar. Stir and cook for about three minutes.

4. Add vegetable stock. If you have a rotary hand blender, use it to puree soup until relatively smooth (or puree in batches in food processor fitted with steel blade).

5. Stir in cream or half and half and tomatoes paste. Reduce heat and simmer for 10 minutes.

6. If you desire the sour cream garnish, mix sour cream with milk. You can place a dollop on top, or place in a squirt bottle and swirl over the top. Then garnish with julienne basil or chopped chives.

Frankie's Tips:

♦ There are a variety of methods you can use to char or roast peppers.... a broiler, a barbecue, or even an open flame. To roast in the broiler or barbecue, cut the peppers in three to four pieces' remove the stem and seeds, flatten out pieces, and then toss with a little olive oil. To broil, place skin-side up on a baking sheet and broil until skin is mostly blackened and peppers are soft— about 7 to 10 minutes. If grilling on a barbecue, place the peppers skin-side down directly over hot flame or coals. Alternately, you can char peppers over an open flame of a gas range burner by holding with tongs and turning as the pepper blackens.

♦ I prefer the flavor of the fresh roasted peppers but you can also use roasted red peppers which come in a jar. For this recipe you would substitute two 16 ounce jars. Rinse before using as most of them are packed in vinegar for preserving.

Creamy Tomato-Gorgonzola Soup
with Pancetta

Remember the soul-warming Tomato Soup you had as a kid? This is a delicious, adult version of that. The soup can be made with the addition of either bleu cheese or gorgonzola, which is essentially the Italian version of bleu cheese. It has a slightly greener tint to it and is a little less piquant to my taste, yet still very similar. Either way it adds a wonderful layer of flavor to the soup.

6 servings

2 tablespoons olive oil

1/2 medium onion--diced

1 large carrot--diced

2 tablespoons fresh garlic--minced

1/2 teaspoon pepper

1 teaspoon salt

28 ounce can crushed tomatoes

2 cups chicken stock

2 tablespoons basil pesto

2 cups heavy cream

3/4 cup Gorgonzola (or Bleu) cheese--crumbled (plus additional for garnish)

3/4 cup pancetta or bacon--pre-cooked and chopped (plus additional for garnish)

1. Heat oil in soup pot. Add diced onion and carrot. Sauté until tender, about 4 to 5 minutes.

2. Add garlic, salt and pepper. Sauté for one minute.

3. Add crushed tomatoes with juices, the chicken stock and basil pesto.

4. If you have a rotary hand blender, use it to puree soup until relatively smooth (or puree soup in batches in food processor fitted with steel blade).

5. Reduce heat and simmer for 8 to 10 minutes. Add heavy cream, gorgonzola cheese and pancetta. Stir and simmer for an additional 8 to 10 minutes.

6. Garnish soup with crumbled gorgonzola and chopped pancetta.

Frankie's Tips:

♦ Sometimes we make this soup without pancetta (though it is not vegetarian unless you substitute vegetable stock for the chicken stock). Whichever variation we prepare, our customers rave whenever we serve it.

♦ If you do not yet own a rotary hand blender, I highly suggest you purchase one. They are inexpensive and a very handy tool to have for making soups and pureed sauces.

Fennnel and Leek Soup
with Potatoes

Fennel is something we tend not to cook much in America but it is gaining in popularity as we broaden our food horizons. In central Italian cooking though, finocchio, as it is called, is a very traditional ingredient.

Fennel can be a little confusing if you're unfamiliar with it because it is both a food plant (looking almost like celery but the bulb part at the base is white); and also as an herb--fennel seed. Both have a flavor similar to anise (think licorice), but that flavor is very subtle in the bulb portion which you use here.

6 servings

3 medium fennel bulbs

2 leeks

1 tablespoon olive oil

1 tablespoon butter

2-3 cloves fresh garlic—minced

1/2 cup white wine

4 cups chicken stock

2 large russet potatoes--peeled and cubed

3/4 cup buttermilk (or light cream)

salt and fresh ground pepper (to taste)

2 tablespoons Sambuca--optional

1. Trim the stems off of the fennel and reserve the feathery leaves from one of the bulbs. Quarter the bulbs lengthwise and then cut out the core at the base and discard. Slice bulbs into medium size pieces.

2. Cut off the base of the leeks and the upper green portion. Slice the white portion lengthwise and rinse under cold water to remove any of the dirt which likes to hide between its layers. Dice into medium sized pieces.

3. Heat butter and olive oil together in a large soup pot over medium-low heat. When butter has melted, add the sliced fennel and leeks. Cook, stirring occasionally until leeks are translucent, about 5 to 10 minutes.

4. Add garlic and stir briefly to release aromatics. Add white wine and cook until reduced by half.

5. Add chicken stock and potatoes. Increase heat to medium-high and bring to a boil. Reduce heat and simmer until potatoes are very soft, about 25 minutes.

6. Using a potato masher, gently mash the vegetables until the soup is thick and chunky; or alternately use a rotary hand blender to lightly puree the soup.

7. Add buttermilk, and then salt and pepper to taste. Chop fronds from reserved fennel stems and add 2 to 3 tablespoons to soup to achieve desired flavor (fronds have a more pronounced fennel flavor than the bulb). Add Sambuca if desired (see Frankie's Tips).

Frankie's Tips:

♦ I love lamb, so when developing this recipe, I had envisioned adding ground lamb to it to create a heartier soup. After trying it though, I personally preferred it without, because I thought the lamb overwhelmed the subtle, yet wonderful flavors. But my wife and daughter preferred it with the lamb. So what do I know!? You could also consider other meats such as sausage, bacon or pancetta.

♦ Another variation which is not uncommon is to add a tablespoon or two of Sambuca, which is an Italian, Anise flavored liqueur. This is a good option if you would like to enhance that flavor profile of anise, which as mentioned in the intro is very similar to fennel.

Fisherman's Soup
Cacciuccio

This soup finds it's origins in the Tuscan coastal town of Livorno, where it's been made for centuries using fresh local fish. Variations appear all over coastal Italy. Traditionally it is made with at least five types of fish and shellfish, one for each "c" in its name.

This soup recipe may look intimidating because of the long list of ingredients, but once you've done the shopping, the preparation is simple.

6 servings

3 tablespoon cup olive oil

1 medium onion—finely chopped

1 stalk celery—finely chopped

2 cloves minced garlic

1/4 cup fresh Italian Parsley—chopped

1-1/2 tablespoons fresh rosemary—chopped fine

pinch of saffron (optional)

pinch dried crushed red pepper

1-1/2 tablespoon flour

3/4 cup dry white wine

28 oz. can Whole Peeled Plum Tomatoes—crushed by hand

1 quart water

1 pound fish (such as 8 oz. each of Sea Bass and Orange Roughy)—rough cut into bite size squares

1 pound shellfish (such as 5-6 oz. each of shrimp, scallops, & calamari)

2 teaspoon sea salt

black pepper – fresh ground

1 tablespoon sugar (optional)

1/2 cup half & half or cream (optional)

6 slices toasted rustic bread (small enough to fit in bottom of bowls)

additional chopped Italian Parsley and Extra Virgin olive oil for garnish

1. Put on some Italian music. Frankie's recommendation: the sound track from *Il Postino*.

2. Heat the olive oil in a large pot over medium heat until it begins to shimmer. Add onion and celery and sauté about 7 minutes, until it begins to soften. Add garlic and sauté an additional 3 minutes.

3. Stir in herbs and crushed red peppers. Sauté about 2 minutes. Add flour and sauté one minute.

4. Add wine and cook until most of the liquid evaporates (this step is known as deglazing). Scrape the browned bits from the bottom of the pot.

5. Add the tomatoes with their juices. Add water. Bring to a boil. Reduce heat and simmer for 20 minutes.

6. Add all seafood to soup. Increase heat to low-medium and cook 3 to 5 minutes until seafood is cooked through, (as seen by opaque color).

7. Add salt and several twists of fresh ground black pepper. Add optional sugar and half & half if desired. Taste and adjust seasoning to your liking.

8. Place a slice of toasted bread in the bottom of each serving bowl. Ladle soup over. Garnish with parsley and drizzle with Extra Virgin olive oil.

Sorrento, Campania

Frankie's Tips:

♦ This recipe is very flexible. I used two types of fish and a Seafood Blend from Trader Joe's which contains shrimp, bay scallops and calamari rings. For the fish, any thick cuts of firm fish will work well. For the shellfish, if you want to use clams or mussels in their shells, as part of your shellfish blend, you will need to purchase triple the weight to compensate for the weight of the shells.

♦ Italians generally do not mix dairy with seafood, thus my optional half & half (or cream) goes outside of tradition. However, I really like the extra layer of savory flavor it adds.

♦ I added a little saffron to my soup and liked the flavor enhancement. Saffron can be added to a cup of the water and heated to dissolve it, or you can crush the threads with a mortar and pestle, or use a simple method of placing it on a cutting board and crushing it with the side of a chef's knife.

Tuscan Bread Salad

In Tuscany, as in other parts of Italy, leftover bread rarely goes to waste. This tradition hearkens back to the days when poverty made it a necessity to use every morsel. The Italians, being a crafty sort, developed many delicious ways to use their old bread, including this heavenly salad.

4-5 servings

Vinaigrette Dressing:

3 tablespoons red wine (or Sherry) vinegar

juice of 1 medium lemon

1 teaspoon Dijon mustard

2 cloves garlic-pressed

2/3 cup extra virgin olive oil

1/2 teaspoon salt

fresh ground black pepper—several grinds

Salad:

4 cups day-old rustic Italian bread—cut into 1 inch cubes

2-1/2 cups cherry tomatoes (consider using both red cherry tomatoes and yellow teardrop tomatoes)

1 small red onion—cut into thin slivers

3 tablespoons chopped Italian parsley

2 cups fresh salad greens or arugula

shaved Parmigiano-Reggiano

1. If your bread is too fresh, cut it up early and let it sit for a few hours, or put the cut up bread on a tray in a slightly warm oven to speed the process.

2. In a large mixing bowl, whisk together the dressing ingredients. Reserve about 3 tablespoons of the dressing and set aside.

3. Add the bread to the large mixing bowl with the dressing. Toss well and let sit for 20 to 30 minutes.

4. Add the tomatoes, red onion, parsley and remaining dressing and toss. Taste and adjust seasoning to your liking.

5. Spread salad greens on a serving platter. Place bread atop salad greens. Top with shaved Parmigiano Reggiano and serve.

Frankie's Tips:

♦ I've thoroughly researched traditional Bread Salads and found that there are many other ingredients which are frequently used. Feel free to add any of these that suit your fancy…

♦ Calamata or other olives (such as Nicoise)

♦ Chopped cucumber

♦ Capers (drained and rinsed of brine)

♦ Fresh basil

♦ Garbonzo beans

♦ Hard boiled eggs

♦ Shaved Ricotta Salata cheese (which is a pressed, salted and dried version of ricotta), to replace the Parmigiano-Reggiano

♦ You can even turn this into an entrée salad by adding tuna (I would recommend the good white tuna in the foil pouch) or by adding pancetta (Italian style bacon) or regular bacon chopped and crumbled over the top.

Insalata Caprese

This is our take on a traditional Caprese salad. The salad originates from the beautiful isle of Capri, located off the Amalfi Coast of southern Italy. A typical version has fresh tomatoes with creamy fresh mozzarella, leaves of fresh basil and a drizzle of extra virgin olive oil. We love the visual appeal of stacking the salad and have added a couple of ingredients; a spoonful of fresh basil pesto and a garnish of balsamic glaze on the plate, which adds another flavor dimension and looks gorgeous.

We serve this each summer at the restaurant and it is a huge hit. People are sad when it goes away in the fall but its just not right unless made with fresh, ripe summer tomatoes.

4 servings

Balsamic Glaze:

1 cup balsamic vinegar

1 tablespoon brown sugar

Salad:

4 large ripe tomatoes--preferably two yellow and two red

2 - 4 ounce balls fresh mozzarella

4 ounces fresh basil pesto

4 sprigs fresh basil-- kissed by the sun

Frankie's Tips:

♦ There are really just a couple of keys to making this salad great. The first is to use fresh, fully ripened tomatoes. Heirloom tomatoes are a wonderful option, though sometimes not as pretty.

♦ And the most flavorful fresh mozzarella you can buy is buffalo milk mozzarella, which is made from water buffalo. It is usually available at Trader Joe's and Costco.

Preparing Balsamic Glaze:

1. To prepare balsamic vinegar glaze, place the vinegar in a small sauce pan over medium-high heat. Whisk regularly until it begins to simmer.

2. Whisk in brown sugar. Reduce heat to low-medium and simmer, whisking regularly until reduced by about two-thirds. It should have a syrupy consistency and coat the back of a spoon. Pour into a small container (or a squirt bottle if you have one). Cool at room temperature. It will thicken more as it cools.

Preparing Salad:

1. You will need 12 slices of fresh mozzarella. With a sharp knife, slice the ends off of the mozzarella balls. Slice remaining portions into 6 slices each.

2. You will need 16 tomato slices. With a sharp knife, slice the ends off of tomatoes. Slice remaining into 4 slices each.

3. With a spoon or squirt bottle, make a design with the balsamic glaze on the outer portion of the plate. Place a tomato slice in middle, then layer alternating slices of fresh mozzarella with red and yellow tomatoes.

4. Top with a tablespoon of basil pesto, allowing it to drip down one side of the stack.

5. Garnish with a sprig of fresh basil.

6. Get out your camera and take a picture. If you post it on-line, everybody will want to come to your house for dinner!

Summer Seasonal Salad
With Strawberries, Candied-Walnuts and Gorgonzola Cheese

This salad speaks of early summer, when strawberries are ripe and juicy. Locally grown strawberries, which show up in June-July, would be the very best. The dressing is a little sweeter (from honey), than the Basil-Vinaigrette which we use on the Chopped Salad. This works well with the fruit and candied walnuts.

Candied Walnuts:

Note: This recipe makes extra nuts so you'll have extra to snack on

1 pound walnut halves or large pieces

1 large egg white

1/2 teaspoon vanilla

1/2 cup sugar

Balsamic-Vinaigrette Dressing:

3 tablespoons balsamic vinegar

2 teaspoons Dijon mustard

3 teaspoons honey

3/4 cup extra virgin olive oil

1/2 teaspoon salt

fresh ground pepper—several grinds

one strong arm for whisking

Salad:

1 part romaine lettuce

1 part mixed seasonal greens

fresh strawberries--stems removed and sliced

gorgonzola cheese--crumbled

Preparing Candied Walnuts:

1. Pre-heat oven to 350 F with oven rack in middle. Lightly oil a rimmed baking pan (or place a Silpat mat on it).

2. Beat egg white and vanilla in a large bowl until frothy. Add nuts and toss to coat.

3. Add sugar and toss to coat. Using a slotted spoon, spread onto baking sheet in a single layer.

4. Bake in oven, stirring once or twice, until dry and well toasted, about 20 minutes. Loosen on the tray and allow to cool to room temperature. Store extra nuts in a plastic bag or covered container.

Preparing Balsamic-Vinaigrette Dressing:

1. Place all ingredients (except for the strong arm), in a mixing bowl.

2. Use the strong arm to whisk until emulsified (blended well together).

Preparing Salad:

1. In a large mixing bowl, toss lettuces with enough vinaigrette to coat to your liking. Save remainder for another use.

2. Transfer to a beautiful serving bowl or platter.

3. Top with strawberries, walnuts and gorgonzola cheese.

Frankie's Tips:

♦ This salad is also excellent with any fresh summer berries such as blueberries, raspberries or blackberries. You can also add kiwi's along with the strawberries for a fun alternative.

♦ If you are not crazy about gorgonzola (which is like Bleu cheese), you can substitute any soft cheese such as feta or goat cheese, or even queso fresco.

Autumn Seasonal Salad
With Apples, Dried-Cranberries and Orange-Ginger Walnuts

This salad tastes like autumn to me. The nuts are simple to make and I've made the recipe for a whole pound so you will have extra for snacking on. Feel free to substitute pecans which are equally delicious, or to buy candied nuts in the store if you want to save time.

Note that I have not listed quantities for the salad ingredients. This is so you can be completely flexible in the size of the salad you make. The dressing will make more than a cup which is more than you need. It will store well in the refrigerator for a couple of weeks. Whisk again before using.

Orange-Ginger Candied Nuts

1 pound walnut halves or large pieces

1 large egg white

1/2 teaspoon vanilla

1/2 cup sugar

1/4 teaspoon ground ginger

2 tablespoons orange zest
(one orange should provide ample zest)

Sherry-Vinaigrette Dressing

3/4 cup extra virgin olive oil

1/4 cup Sherry vinegar

1 tablespoons honey

2 teaspoons Dijon mustard

1/2 teaspoon salt

Fresh ground black pepper
—several twists

A strong arm for whisking

Autumn Salad

1 part mixed seasonal greens

1 part romaine lettuce--chopped

apples—cut into large bite size pieces
(I like Gala apples for this)

lemon juice—optional
(see Frankie's Tips)

dried cranberries

gorgonzola cheese—crumbled

Preparing Orange-Ginger Candied Nuts:

1. Pre-heat oven to 350 F with rack in middle. Lightly oil a rimmed baking pan (or place a Silpat mat on it).

2. Beat egg white and vanilla in a large bowl until frothy. Add nuts and toss to coat.

3. Combine the sugar, ginger and orange zest in a bowl and mix together. Sprinkle over nuts and toss to coat. Using a slotted spoon, spread onto baking sheet in a single layer.

4. Bake in oven, stirring once or twice, until dry and well toasted, about 20 minutes. Loosen on the tray and allow to cool to room temperature. Store extra nuts in a plastic bag or covered container.

Preparing Sherry-Vinaigrette:

1. Place all ingredients (except for the strong arm), in a mixing bowl.

2. Use the strong arm to whisk until emulsified (blended well together).

Preparing Salad:

1. In a large mixing bowl, toss your favorite mixed salad greens with enough vinaigrette to coat to your liking.

2. Transfer to a beautiful (preferably shallow) serving bowl or platter.

3. Top with apples, cranberries, gorgonzola cheese, and candied nuts.

4. Thank your creator for this beautiful and healthy salad!

Frankie's Tips:

♦ In this salad, I recommend tossing only the salad greens with the dressing. This is because I like the gorgeous appearance of all of the fresh apples and other ingredients atop the salad. That is also why I suggest a shallow bowl or platter for presenting it. If you use a deeper bowl, I recommend you fill it half full of tossed greens, and then place a layer of the other ingredients, and then the remaining greens and ingredients atop that. Otherwise the first people to attack the bowl will get all the goodies.

♦ When preparing the candied walnuts, if you would prefer to use fresh ginger instead of dried, use one full teaspoon.

♦ At the restaurant we've tasted various apples. I like Gala for their color, flavor, and texture; and we have found they do not brown as quickly when they are cut up. If you want to cut your apples in advance however, I recommend that you toss them in lemon juice and water (one part Lemon juice to two parts water). The acid in the lemon juice will keep the fruit from turning brown.

Chopped Antipasto Salad

We do not serve a "chopped" salad at the restaurant. We get many requests for it but our salad prep area is just too small. But like many people, I love my salad prepared this way, so I decided to do it in that fashion for the cook book. The only real difference of course is that the ingredients are chopped small before being tossed together. Buon appetito!

Basil-Vinaigrette Dressing:

1/4 cup balsamic vinegar

1 cup extra virgin olive oil

1 tablespoon water

1/2 teaspoon fresh garlic

1 tablespoon dried basil

1 teaspoon salt

1/4 teaspoon sugar

1 teaspoon Dijon mustard

fresh ground black pepper—several grinds

one strong arm for whisking

Salad Ingredients:

2 parts romaine lettuce--chopped

1 part mixed seasonal greens--chopped

fresh diced tomatoes

red onion—finely diced

garbonzo beans

artichoke hearts (canned or frozen) -- cut up small

olives (your favorite or mixed)

salami--cut into small cubes

provolone or mozzarella cheese-- cut into small cubes

pepperocini peppers

Preparing Basil-Vinaigrette Dressing:

1. Place all ingredients (except for the strong arm), in a mixing bowl.

2. Use the strong arm to whisk until emulsified (blended well together).

Preparing Salad:

1. In a large mixing bowl, toss all ingredients (except pepperocinis) with enough vinaigrette to coat to your liking.

2. Transfer to a beautiful (preferably shallow) serving bowl or platter.

3. Top with Pepperocini peppers.

4. Move out of the way so you don't get trampled by the hungry mob!

Frankie's Tips:

♦ For the lettuce, I recommended 2 parts romaine to 1 part mixed seasonal greens. Vary this to your liking. If changing anything though, I would probably add more romaine, because you want a crisp, firm base for this salad. Ice berg lettuce would also work okay but lacks the nutritional value of romaine. Crisp radicchio would also be a nice addition for both texture and color.

♦ The dressing will likely make more than you need. It will store well in the refrigerator for a couple of weeks though. Whisk again before using.

Rhonda's Smoked Salmon & Caper Sandwich

I must give credit for this to my wife who first started making these sandwiches last summer. Any smart man of course would put his wife's recipe in his cook book! The reality is that this is a really good sandwich and deserves a spot.

Rhonda usually makes these on whole wheat bagels, but you can use any bread you like. They would be excellent on thick focaccia bread, on a Ciabatta, or on thickly sliced and grilled Italian Bread.

Serves 2 or more

bread of choice (see notes above)

Aioli (recipe page 68) or mayonnaise
—approximately 1 rounded teaspoon
per sandwich

mustard (preferably Dijon)—about 1
teaspoon per sandwich (optional)

capers—approximately 1 teaspoon per
sandwich—rinsed of brine and drained

butter to spread

garlic powder

mozzarella (or other favorite cheese)
--sliced

smoked salmon—approximately 3
ounces per sandwich

fresh dill—one or two sprigs per
sandwich

lettuce (preferably butterhead)

tomato—2 to 3 slices per sandwich

A kiss from the one you love

1. Set oven Broiler on low setting.

2. Mix together aioli, mustard and capers (adjust ratio to your liking).

3. Spread bread lightly with butter and sprinkle lightly with garlic powder. Place cheese on one side of bread and salmon on the opposite side.

4. Place open faced under broiler until cheese is bubbly and salmon is warm.

5. Top salmon with mayonnaise, mustard, and caper blend. Top with fresh dill. Add lettuce and tomato atop opposite side.

Frankie's Tips:

♦ You can serve the salmon either warm or cold with this. If you prefer it cold, simply wait to add it until after you broil the open face bread and cheese.

♦ Last time I made this I smoked my own salmon on the grill. This works best with real charcoal or even better with real wood lump charcoal. Move your hot coals to one side to create indirect heat and place salmon fillets skin side down on the opposite side of the grill. Add smoker chips (alder works nice). Reduce air to accomplish a low heat and cook until fish loses translucence.

Foccacia Caprese Sandwich

My wife and I took a day trip to the Isle of Capri in 2004, having taken the ferry from Positano on the Amalfi coast of Italy. It's a magical place and the food is simple, but oh so delectable! We decided then that someday we would return for a longer visit.

It was not long afterward; inspired by the Insalata Caprese, a salad made with fresh mozzarella, deliciously ripe tomatoes and fresh basil, that I created this sandwich for the restaurant. It is one of my favorite things on the menu, especially for lunch. My favorite way to eat it is with a little thinly sliced prosciutto added, which we make available as a menu option at Frankie's.

Serves 2 or more

thick foccacia bread or Ciabatta bread-- about 4x5 inches

mayonnaise--1 teaspoon per sandwich

basil pesto--3/4 teaspoon per sandwich

tomato—2 to 3 slices per sandwich

fresh mozzarella--2 oz. per sandwich-- cut into 3-4 slices (see Frankie's Tip's)

prosciutto--1/2 ounce per sandwich-- sliced thin (optional)

fresh basil leaves

Frankie's Tips:

♦ We serve this on thick foccacia bread, but Ciabatta bread would also work great. You could also grill it on a panini grill or pan if you have one.

♦ Fresh mozzarella, also known as Fior Di Latte, is different than regular mozzarella. It is fresher, softer, and far more perishable than regular mozzarella. It also has a higher moisture content. For more information, see the notes about cheeses under *Pizza Ingredients (page 74)*.

1. Turn on oven broiler.
2. Blend mayonnaise and pesto together to make a pesto-mayonnaise (this is wonderful for any sandwich!).
3. Slice open foccacia bread. Lay open face. Spread pesto mayonnaise onto one side of bread.
4. Layer tomato slices atop pesto mayo (2 to 3 slices depending on size). Layer fresh mozzarella atop tomatoes.
5. If adding prosciutto, place atop bread opposite the tomatoes and fresh mozzarella.
6. Broil until cheese begins to melt.
7. Garnish sandwich with a sprig of fresh basil.
8. As you take your first bite, close your eyes and feel the warm Mediterranean sun upon your face as you gaze upon the most beautiful azure water you have ever laid eyes on.

Pesto Chicken Sandwich

The dressing for this sandwich is made by blending fresh basil pesto with mayonnaise, which is delicious. It could also be done with sun-dried tomato pesto which is equally delightful. I mentioned in my pesto recipes that I like to freeze them in small plastic containers, so I bring out just the amount I need. You can even freeze it in ice trays and then transfer the frozen pesto cubes to a zip lock freezer bag.

Serves 2 or more

thick foccacia bread or Ciabatta bread--about 4x5 inches

mayonnaise--1-1/2 teaspoons per sandwich

basil pesto--1 teaspoon per sandwhich

sliced provolone cheese--one or two slices

roasted chicken breast--approximately 4 ounces--1 per sandwich (see Frankie's Tip's)

roasted red peppers

red onion--sliced thin

fresh basil (optional--for garnish)

1. Turn on oven broiler.
2. Blend mayonnaise and pesto together to make a pesto-mayonnaise.
3. Slice open foccacia or Ciabatta bread. Lay open face. Spread pesto mayonnaise onto one side of bread.
4. Place provolone cheese atop pesto mayo. Layer roasted red peppers and red onions atop cheese.
5. Place chicken breast on opposite side.
6. Place open faced under broiler until cheese is bubbly and chicken is warm.
7. Garnish sandwich with a julienne of fresh basil.

Frankie's Tips:

♦ I like my chicken sliced thin on this sandwich. When we serve it at the restaurant, we slice the breast in half to achieve two thin breasts. Be careful so you do not cut yourself.

♦ For the roasted red peppers, you can roast them yourselves if you desire (see note on "how to" under the *Pizza Ingredients--page 76*). You can also purchase them in a jar. Use the leftovers in pasta or on pizza. They are also great on salads.

Italian BLT

This sandwich, which is modeled after a traditional BLT, is probably my favorite sandwich in the whole world. The main difference from a BLT, is that it has pancetta, an Italian-style bacon, instead of regular bacon. I adore pancetta. It is not smoked like regular bacon but has more spiciness to it. We added this sandwich to our lunch menu at Frankie's. I thought it would be a great seller but sadly it sold so poorly that we took it off the menu a few months later. If only people knew what they were missing!

Serves 2 or more

1 loaf rustic Italian bread
or French baguette--sliced

sliced pancetta--3 to 4 slices per
sandwich--cooked like bacon

tomato—2 to 3 slices per sandwich

arugula or mixed seasonal greens

Aioli (see Preparing Aioli--bottom right)

1. Prepare aioli or "faux" aioli (see below).
2. Grill pancetta.
3. Lightly oil the bread and pan (or grill). Place pancetta and aioli on sandwich. If you do not have a panini grill or pan, grill the sandwich in a skillet (cast iron would be next best thing), as you would a grilled cheese.
4. Place tomato slices and arugula greens atop pancetta.
5. Its okay to moan in rapturous delight as you eat this sandwich. The person you are with will probably be doing the same.

Frankie's Tips:

♦ Pancetta generally comes in a roll form so when sliced, it provides round or oval slices which are 3 to 4 inches in diameter, perfect for sandwiches. You may not find pancetta in all grocery stores, but most specialty food stores like Whole Foods will carry it, as well as many butcher shops. If they do not have it pre-sliced, ask if they can slice it for you.

♦ Arugula, also known as *rocket (or rochette)*, is a spicy, somewhat bitter green which goes perfect with this sandwich.

♦ An option on this is to grill it Panini style with a Panini pan or counter-top Panini grill.

Preparing Aioli:

Aioli is a wonderful, garlicky mayonnaise of French origin. It can be made very basic, as it is here, or many variations can be made by adding things such as: puree of roasted red pepper, or some Basil Pesto or Sun-dried Tomato Pesto. It is fairly simple to make from scratch. But if raw egg scares you, or if you want to keep it really simple, you can make "faux" aioli by adding crushed garlic and lemon juice (to taste) to mayonnaise with just a touch of extra salt.

To prepare aioli from scratch, in a blender or food processor, you need the following ingredients:

1 egg
3/4 teaspoon salt
2-3 cloves of garlic--crushed
1 heaping teaspoon Dijon mustard
1 cup oil (olive oil, or canola, or half & half)
1 tablespoon hot water
1 tablespoon lemon juice
1 tablespoon white wine vinegar

Place egg, salt, garlic, and mustard in blender with about 1/8 cup of the oil. Start blender and add remaining oil in a slow, steady stream. Then add hot water. Turn off blender. Scrape into a bowl and stir in lemon juice and vinegar.

A special thanks to Andy, our executive chef at Frankie's. Andy was a tremendous help to me; testing recipes, and breaking down many of our large restaurant recipes to "human size". This often involved going shopping to see what sizes of products were available and then re-testing the recipes.

Andy Rafferty - Executive Chef

Civita di Bagnoregio, Umbria

Pizza e Calzones

Making Pizza at Home

Making pizza from scratch takes time, but if you have that time it's very fun and rewarding! There are alternatives to doing things completely from scratch. One is to purchase pizza dough from your favorite pizzeria (Frankie's of course, if you are in the area). Most places will sell it—we even bought some in Tuscany on our last trip so we could make pizza in the wood burning oven at the house we were renting. The advantage of dough from a pizzeria is that it is made from flour specially formulated for pizza, providing optimum elasticity and pliability, which makes it easier to stretch and it does not tear as easily. Another option is to buy pre-made bread dough, which some grocery stores sell.

If buying dough at your pizzeria, see if they sell their sauce as well. Or you can buy canned sauce at a grocery store. The advantage is convenience, but homemade pizza sauce is quick and easy to prepare.

If you're visiting a high quality pizzeria like Frankie's, you could also consider buying some of their mozzarella cheese. The mozzarella we purchase at the restaurant is better than any I've found in the grocery stores.

Yet do not be daunted from making pizza from scratch. You can make the dough and sauce in the morning, or better still the day before, and the rest is easy. Imagine your pride as you pull those hot, bubbly pies from the oven! And you will be a hero to your family.

Tools and how to use them:

Stand Mixer with Dough Hook (or large capacity Food Processor): Personally, I prefer a stand mixer over a food processor for making pizza dough. You will need a dough hook, as beaters do not work well for mixing dough. Use according to the pizza dough recipe.

Pizza Stone: Unless you use a pizza stone, you will not be able to get the quality results you find in a great pizzeria like Frankie's. A pizza stone, if heated properly, will seal the bottom of the pizza crust quickly, providing superior texture and crispness. A pizza stone can be purchased at any good kitchen store. Sometimes you can find them packaged with a wooden pizza peel.

By the way, pizza stones are great for baking rustic breads as well. And one other good use… if you ever do take out pizza, and want it to be as fresh and hot as it is at the pizzeria, ask them to "half-bake" it and leave it uncut. Bring it home and finish it on your stone. Your family will fall down and worship you!

How to use: In order for your pizza stone to work properly you need to get it really hot! I recommend a minimum of 45 minutes at 500° F (if your oven will go that high). One note though—if you plan to put a lot of toppings on your pizza, reduce the temperature to about 485 F, or the bottom of the pizza will get overcooked by the time the toppings and cheese are properly cooked.

Alternatives to a Pizza Stone?: I personally believe that a pizza stone is the best way to cook pizza at home, unless you are making a deep dish-style pizza (you will find one later this chapter--done in a cast iron skillet). You can purchase a pizza stone for about $30 (or much more). If this is beyond your budget, or you're just plain desperate, the next best alternative in my mind is a cast iron skillet. If you have neither, you can use a pan. To do so, oil it lightly before you put the dough on it, and reduce your oven temperature to 450° F. The bake time will be more along the lines of 15 minutes.

Wooden Pizza Peel: In order to safely get your pizza on and off of your pizza stone, you will need a pizza peel. Most pizzerias use two types of peels, a wooden peel for putting pizzas into the oven, and a metal peel for removing them. You could do that at home, but one wooden peel will be adequate for both purposes. Metal pizza peels are only designed for *removing* pizzas from the oven. They do not work well with raw dough because it sticks to the metal much more so than wood. For home use, a wooden peel is adequate for both purposes.

How to use: You will be placing your stretched dough on the pizza peel prior to topping your pizza. Otherwise it is nearly impossible to transfer the topped pizza onto the board for placing in the oven.

Very important! You will need to sprinkle the wooden peel with cornmeal or a coarse flour (at Frankie's we use a coarse Semolina Flour), before placing your dough on it. This will prevent the dough from sticking to the peel, and act as mini-rollers for helping you slide the pizza onto the pizza stone.

Another important note regarding this: the longer you leave the dough on the pizza peel, the more it will tend to stick to the board. So place the dough on the board, and then top immediately and place pizza in oven. If doing a second pizza on the same stone, wait until the first is out of the oven before you start the second. This is partly so it is not on the pizza peel too long, but also you will need the peel to remove the first pizza from the oven (unless you have two).

Pizza Ingredients:

One thing that makes pizza so much fun is that you can put just about anything on it you like. Don't hesitate to experiment. Here are a few notes for your consideration.

Mozzarella: Mozzarella of course is the most traditional cheese for topping pizza. It melts wonderfully, has great elasticity, and a mild flavor which nicely complements the other ingredients. One of the problems is that it is hard to find brands in the grocery store which are as good as what we have available in the restaurant.

When most of you think of Mozzarella, you think of standard Mozzarella, often pre-shredded—but it comes in many forms. Let's examine the options...

Whole Milk vs Part-Skim: Whole Milk Mozzarella has more fat of course, which makes it richer, creamier; and well just plain better in my opinion. The down side of course is the extra calories (though if you compare them you'll be surprised how small the difference can be). Part Skim Mozzarella is adequate but you give up some flavor and texture.

Whole Block vs Pre-Shredded: Whether you buy whole milk or part-skim, I highly recommend that you buy cheese in whole block form (as opposed to pre-shredded). Grocery store brands of pre-shredded cheeses generally contain an anti-caking agent which contains cellulose and other non-natural ingredients that I cannot pronounce. It may save a few minutes but it is not worth the convenience in my opinion.

Fresh Mozzarella—Cow's Milk vs Mozzarella di Bufala: Fresh Mozzarella (also known as Fior Di Latte) is fresher, softer, and far more perishable than regular Mozzarella. It also has a higher moisture content. It is stored in a brine and generally only has a shelf life of about a week (though it can be frozen). This is the perfect cheese for Insalata Caprese. I also love it on pizza, though I find some brands to be bland. If using for pizza, you should place it on a paper towel and roll it around to remove as much moisture as possible, or else you will have a wet pizza. Then cut in thin slices or break it up.

Mozzarella di Bufala (also known as Burrata) is made from the extra rich milk of a Water Buffalo. It is the best Mozzarella in the world in my humble opinion! On my visits to Italy, I made sure to search it out. Many pizzerias sell it, but only upon special request. It is only recently becoming available in this country. In the Seattle area it can be found at Costco, Trader Joe's and high-end grocery stores or Italian markets. Even in Italy it costs more, but in this country it is very high priced, since much of it is produced in Italy and flown over because of its short shelf life. There are now a few people beginning to produce it in the states. Because of its high cost, I don't use it all the time, but do like to splurge on occasion.

Other Cheeses: Any semi-soft cheese is great for pizza. Some of my favorites are Provolone, Fontina, Smoked Mozzarella, Gouda and Cheddar. I generally blend these with mozzarella for best results. Other cheeses I enjoy are Gorgonzola, Feta, and Goat cheeses. In my opinion though, these are best when used sparingly and with other mild cheeses to soften their pungency. I also love a little Ricotta when used in conjunction with other cheeses.

Harder cheeses such as Parmesan and Pecorino Romano will not melt well if used by themselves, but they will melt fine if blended with softer cheeses. Both can add a nice layer of flavor. If you like things a little salty, Pecorino Romano is an excellent choice.

Pizza Ingredients:

Flour: The advantage of flour used in a pizzeria is that it is especially formulated for pizza, providing optimum elasticity and pliability. It is much easier to work with than any brand of flour found on grocery store shelves. It's worth asking at your favorite pizzeria to see if they might sell you some (Frankie's of course if you live in the area). The second best alternative I have found is called "00" flour which is usually imported from Italy. I have been unable to find it in local grocery stores. But I had great results with a brand called *Antimo Caputo* from Napoli which I purchased on-line (see info on right).

A great on-line source for "00" flour and pizza equipment is FG Pizza & Italian Supplies at www.fgpizza.com.

As far as grocery store brand flours, we tested several in an attempt to match our own dough recipe as closely as possible. The one which worked best in our trials was *Stone Buhr Bread Flour.* It was the easiest to stretch and had the best flavor profile. Interestingly, none of the other bread flours we tested provided satisfactory results (very tough dough); so if you don't have Stone Buhr Bread Flour available, I recommend using an All Purpose Flour, all of which yielded fairly comparable results to one another.

Sauces: In Italy, the most commonly used sauces are Tomato Sauce, Basil Pesto, or just simply olive oil and tomatoes (which is used on one of Italy's most traditional pizzas—the Pizza Margherita). The tomato sauces used in Italy tends to be thinner and more lightly spiced than what we are used to here. At Frankie's, other sauces we use include Sun-dried Tomato Pesto, and a Garlic-Cream Sauce.

For some of our pizzas, like our Pizza Margherita, we use canned San Marzano-style tomatoes (see explanation on page 14). We place these in a colander, roughly crush them by hand, add a little salt, and drain them very well. These are then scattered atop the dough in place of sauce. This makes a great combination with Fresh Mozzarella; but beware—if you do not drain both the tomatoes and the cheese well, you will end up with a wet pizza pie.

Another tradition common to Italy is to lightly drizzle the top of the pizza with a good Extra Virgin Olive Oil after it comes out of the oven. I highly recommend this practice.

Meats: The most commonly used meats in Italy are dried-cured meats such as Pepperoni, Prosciutto, Pancetta, and various Salamis of which there are dozens of variations. Italian Sausage is also very popular—both in its sweet and spicy form.

Regarding Sausage: We pre-cook our sausage at the restaurant which allows us to drain off the additional fat; and so the staff is not handling raw meats while topping pizzas (which for us is a food safety decision). You can pre-cook it if you prefer or leave it raw. If using it raw, the fatty juices will drain off on your pizza. This additional fat will provide great flavor but will yield a greasier pie. If you are using it raw, make sure to crumble it small enough so it will cook through completely. If you decide to pre-cook it, the easiest way is to do so in a sauté pan—using a wooden spoon to crumble it as it cooks--until all pink is gone. Then pour off the extra fat, and allow the sausage to cool down, prior to use.

Beyond these meats, the sky is the limit. Chicken, meatballs, ground beef, and ham or Canadian Bacon are all popular choices in the states. Bacon is also yummy, as is its Italian cousin, pancetta (which is cured but not smoked and is a little spicier than bacon).

Pizza Ingredients:

Vegetables: Once again, only your imagination limits the possibilities here. I have a few tips below for you to consider.

Using fresh vegetables: At Frankie's we use most of our vegetables fresh. Just keep in mind that they will give off some water. The more you use, the wetter the pizza will be. Fresh tomatoes are the worst culprit. To avoid this, slice them thin, or dice and drain them. You can also add sliced, room temperature tomatoes after baking. The residual heat will warm them quickly.

Another thing you can do is place the vegetables under the cheese when baking. They will give off less water and stay crisper, which may or may not be desirable to you.

Generally speaking, I like my vegetables—especially peppers and onions—sliced thin. The flavors are more subtle and they give off less liquid during cooking.

There are some vegetables I like to pre-cook prior to use. I recommend doing this with vegetables that are very crisp, such as broccoli or asparagus. A couple of my other favorites to prepare this way are roasted peppers, and caramelized onions.

Roasted Peppers: You can roast any color pepper of course, or any type of pepper for that matter. At Frankie's we use roasted red peppers on some of our house pizzas. These can be purchased in a jar, if you want to take the easy route, but they are also super easy to roast your self—and the flavor and texture are superior

There are a variety of methods you can use to char or roast peppers: a broiler, a barbecue, or even an open flame. To roast in the broiler or barbecue, cut the peppers in three or four pieces, remove the seeds, flatten the peppers out, and then toss with a little olive oil. To broil, place skin-side up on a baking sheet and broil until skin is mostly blackened and peppers are soft—about 7 to 10 minutes. If grilling on a barbecue, place the peppers skin-side down directly over a hot flame or coals. Alternately, you can char whole peppers over an open flame of a gas range burner by holding with tongs and turning as the pepper blackens.

After roasting, place peppers in a covered container, or a paper or zip lock bag. Allow to cool and "sweat" 10 to 15 minutes. This loosens the skin which then slips off fairly easily (don't worry if some of it does not want to come off—this just adds character). Slice in thin strips.

Various Onions: For most of our pizzas at Frankie's we use raw red or yellow onions placed atop the pizza prior to baking. In the summer we feature a Walla Walla Onion Pizza which is delicious and very popular. Leeks, shallots or green onions are also tasty.

Once in a while for a treat we will make a pizza with caramelized onions. To caramelize onions, place them in a sauté pan with a little oil over medium heat and cook, stirring periodically until a deep, rich, golden-brown. Since they cook down a lot, cook more than you think you need. The leftovers would never get wasted in my house. Some people add sugar to aid the caramelizing process. Personally I do not like the extra sweetness.

Spinach: Many pizza recipes I've seen call for frozen spinach—which must be squeezed dry prior to use. Personally I prefer fresh spinach, but it does not cook well if placed atop the cheese. The solution is to place a layer of spinach underneath the cheese.

Pizza Ingredients:

Mushrooms: When using raw mushrooms atop a pizza, slice them fairly thin so they will cook through. If you desire them to be more substantial, with a meatier texture, slice them thicker, or quarter them and sauté them ahead.

If you want to splurge a little, try some wild mushroom varieties. In the Autumn, we serve a Wild Mushroom pizza at Frankie's. We buy them fresh but another good way to purchase them is in dried form. To prepare dried mushrooms, soak in hot water for 30 minutes—and then drain well and place on paper towels to remove excess moisture before using. If using Shiitakes, cut off the stem, it is very woody.

Garlic: Garlic can be used either fresh or roasted. Since fresh garlic burns fairly easily I suggest placing it under the cheese, or just adding extra garlic to your sauce. For roasted garlic, you can roast entire heads or individual cloves. To roast a whole head—cut off the top to expose the individual cloves, drizzle with olive oil, wrap with foil and roast in a 400° F oven for 30 to 35 minutes until tender and aromatic.

Pizza Dough

The type of flour you use can make a big difference in regards to the pliability and stretchability of your pizza dough, as well as the chewy texture of the finished dough when baked. On page 75, I have discussed the pros and cons of various flours and my recommendations.

This recipe is designed to use a stand mixer with a dough hook. Alternatively you may use a large capacity food processor.

Enough for two 14" pizzas

1 cup warm water (110 degrees)

1 package yeast

1-3/4 teaspoon salt

1-1/2 teaspoon sugar

3-1/4 Cup Flour (Stone Buhr Bread Flour or All Purpose Flour)

2 tablespoons + 1 teaspoon olive oil

1. Gently whisk yeast into warm water and set aside until it becomes slightly foamy on top (indicating the yeast is alive).

2. Place flour, salt and sugar in mixing bowl. Stir together.

3. Add olive oil and yeast water.

4. Mix on speed #1 for 4 minutes with dough hook attachment.

   Note: If the dough does not begin to come together within the first two minutes, add water, one tablespoon at a time until it does.

5. Remove dough and knead briefly by hand.   Place in a large unsealed freezer bag (or oiled and covered bowl) for 15 minutes. Remove ball from bag and form two smooth dough balls. Place in separate storage bags (leave unsealed for now). Allow to rise for at least two hours, then seal the bags and move to refrigerator for up to 2 days.

Frankie's Tips:

♦ I recommend making your pizza dough either the day before (which will yield the best flavor), or in the morning.

♦ Be careful not to overwork your dough or it will be tough .

Pizza Sauce

You can buy canned pizza sauce at the supermarket, but if you make your own, it will taste better. When making sauce with ingredients from the grocery store, we had best results with Tomato Puree, but not all stores carry it. An alternative is to use a good Tomato Sauce. If doing so, refer to Frankie's Tips for the appropriate recipe adjustments.

Enough for two 14" pizzas

1 - 10.75 oz. can Tomato Puree*

2 cloves fresh Garlic—pressed

1 tablespoon fresh Basil—julienned (or 1 teaspoon dried)

1 teaspoon dried Oregano (or 1 tablespoon fresh)

1/2 teaspoon salt (preferably Sea salt)

1/4 teaspoon sugar (or more to your taste)

1-1/2 teaspoon Extra Virgin Olive Oil

1. Place all ingredients in a bowl and stir together. Adjust salt and spices to taste. Refrigerate for up to 3 days.

2. Seems like there should be more but that's it!

Frankie's Tips:

♦ This sauce is at its best if made in advance so the flavors meld together. I suggest making it when you make your pizza dough.

♦ If you are unable to find Tomato Puree, substitute Tomato Sauce. I like Muir Glen Organic, but it comes in a 15 ounce can which will give you a larger batch. Add 3 tablespoons of Tomato Paste to thicken. If you use a 15 ounce can, increase other ingredients by one-half.

How to Make a Pizza:

If you expect to pick up a pizza dough and toss it like a pro—you are probably going to get pretty discouraged. It takes a lot of practice (if you want to practice, lightly dampen a square cloth and practice with that first). On the other hand, with just a little practice you can stretch your dough so it comes out almost round (who cares if its perfect!), and it will taste great.

Pizza Stone Method: highly recommended! (See notes on page 73)

1. Prepare pizza dough and sauce according to recipes.

2. At least 45 minutes prior to baking, place pizza stone on middle rack of oven (with no racks above it) and pre-heat to 500° F (or 485° F if you plan to load your pizza with a lot of toppings, or if you want to make your crust thicker).

3. Remove dough from refrigerator and allow to come to room temperature (20 to 30 minutes).

4. Sprinkle cornmeal or semolina flour on the wooden pizza peel. Sprinkle flour on a work counter for stretching the dough. Place dough on the floured surface. Lightly flour the dough and your hands.

5. Create a round disk out of the dough by rotating the dough with your hands while pressing gently on the sides and top. You want to achieve a round disk, about 3/4 of an inch thick, which is somewhat evenly proportioned and balanced.

6. Now begin to stretch the dough on the counter. Press the dough out with your fingers, rotating as you go to maintain a balanced dough. Then grab the edges of the dough and pull outwards, again rotating as you go, until the dough is less than a half inch thick, (leave the middle just a little thicker or it may stretch too thin later). If at any time the dough is hard to stretch, set it aside and allow to rest for a few minutes. This will relax the glutens and make it more pliable.

7. Now, to create a thicker edge on the dough, place the palm of your hand on the edge of the dough. Then using your fingers, push the edge of the dough towards your palm to create a rim on the dough, rotating the dough as you go (see top photo on page 81).

8. Now, lift the dough and place it over the back of your hands (see photo at right). By pulling outwards with your hands, gently stretch the dough to the size and thickness you like. Do not rush this step, or pull too hard or you will tear the dough. Also, the dough will have a tendency to spring back, so it is best to stretch it a little larger than you want the pizza to be. If you want to try tossing the dough, place it on the back of your hands, cross your hands over, then uncross them quickly while at the same time pushing upwards very quickly.

    Note: Don't fret if you tear the dough while stretching. Just place on a flat surface and close the hole by overlapping the dough and press firmly together.

9. Place the stretched dough on the wooden pizza peel, and give the handle shake back-and-forth to make sure it is not sticking to the board (if it is, you need more cornmeal or semolina flour).

10. Using a ladle or spoon, place pizza sauce (quantity to your liking) on pizza and spread evenly. Then top with your favorite cheeses and toppings.

11. Shake the handle of the pizza peel again to make sure the pizza is not sticking to the board. Then, using your wooden pizza peel, transfer the pizza to your pre-heated pizza stone.

12. Bake until the crust is brown and firm on the edges, and your cheese is fully melted and beginning to brown (about 6 to 8 minutes). Use pizza peel to remove pizza and place on a pizza pan. Slice and serve hot and bubbly!

How to Make a Pizza

Recipes for some of my favorite pizzas begin on the next page

Pizza Margherita

What a better place to start than the most historic pizza on planet earth. In 1889, Rafaele Esposito of the Pizzeria di Pietro e Basta Cosi in Naples (now called Pizzeria Brandi), prepared a special pizza for the visit of King Umberto I and Queen Margherita. In a patriotic fervor, Esposito used red tomato sauce, white mozzarella cheese, and green basil leaves as toppings to mimic the colors of the Italian flag.

Queen Margherita loved the pizza, and what eventually became Pizza Margherita has since become an international standard. Pizzeria Brandi, now more than 200 years old, still proudly displays a royal thank-you note signed by Galli Camillo, "head of the table of the royal household", dated June 1889.

Toppings (in order of assembly):

San Marzano tomatoes--crushed and well drained (or fresh tomatoes--chopped)

mozzarella cheese (if you really want to be authentic, use Mozzarella di Bufala--see note under ingredients, page 74)

extra virgin olive oil (drizzled on top after baking)

fresh basil--leaves torn or julienne cut (also added after baking)

Pizza Bianco

As I have gotten older, my tastes have changed. And one thing I have come to love and appreciate is simplicity in food, including pizza. I still like a pizza with lots of stuff on it. But more often than not, I'd rather keep it simple. This pizza fits the bill. Its one of the simplest, yet tastiest of all pies.

Toppings (in order of assembly):

drizzle extra virgin olive oil on dough

fresh garlic - finely minced or pressed

fresh herbs (such as fresh basil, oregano, or any other favorites

mozzarella cheese

Frankie's Tip: It is best to make sure that you put the fresh herbs under the cheese to keep them from burning. You can also use dried herbs. Also, feel free to try other cheeses.

Quattro Formaggio Pizza

This is another traditional, yet simple pizza. Most recipes call for a red sauce. We've chosen to make ours with fresh basil pesto. You can blend any four cheeses that you like, or vary the ratio to suit your personal tastes. As far as the tomatoes are concerned, I like them to be sliced very thinly.

Toppings (in order of assembly):

basil pesto - brushed generously atop dough

1 cup mozzarella cheese

1/2 cup fontina cheese

1/4 cup parmigiano-reggiano

1/4 cup gorgonzola

thinly sliced roma tomato

Frankie's Tip: The quantity of cheese is to help you with a ratio. If you feel it isn't enough cheese, add a little more.

Wines for pairing:

Suggested Wine with Pizza Margherita: *Primitivo*

DNA studies have shown that Primitivo is the clonal to parent to our American Zinfandel. It was brought to California by Italian immigrants, but for well over a century its heritage had been lost. Primitivo, which hails from Apulia - the heel of Italy's boot, has more spiciness than Zinfandel and is not so jammy in character.

Frankie's recommendation: *Tormaresca "Torcicoda" Primitivo*

Suggested Wine with Pizza Bianco: *Valpolicella Classico*

I was really surprised that a red wine paired best with this pizza. Valpolicella hails from Veneto. It is made from the little known indigenous grapes Corvina, Rondinella, and Molinara. The wine is generally light-bodied, velvety, and zesty.

Frankie's recommendation: *Zenato Valpolicella Classico*

Suggested Wine with Quattro Formaggio: *Vermentino*

The Vermentino grape is grown primarily in two places of Italy. On the island of Sardegna and in the coastal area of Bolgheri in Tuscany, where this version is from. The wine has a personality which really stands out. On the palate it is harmonious, and very persistent, with a delightful minerality.

Frankie's recommendation: *Guado al Tasso Vermentino*

Gourmet Vegetarian Pizza

This pizza has been on our menu from the very beginning and continues to be one of our top sellers. The colors are vibrant and the flavor is so good. I think it is one of my very best creations!

Toppings (in order of assembly):

pizza sauce

mozzarella cheese--about 3/4 of the total

fontina cheese--about 1/4 of the total

artichoke hearts--broken up

red onion--thinly slivered

sun-dried tomatoes

roasted red peppers (if you want to roast your own, see procedure page 76)

calamata olives

fresh basil--leaves torn or julienne cut (added after baking)

Mediterranean Pizza

This pizza is unique and very delish! For the sauce we use our Sun-dried Tomato Pesto. I suggest making a batch, and storing it in small containers in the freezer. That way you'll have it handy for a quick pasta or pizza. It is also great on grilled meats and fish.

Toppings (in order of assembly):

sun-dried tomato pesto (recipe page 112)

mozzarella cheese

goat cheese (light quantity)--scattered

cooked chicken--sliced thin

pancetta--pre-cooked & diced

artichoke hearts--broken up

red onions--slivered

calamata olives

red bell peppers--sliced

fresh basil (after baking)--torn or julienne cut

Frankie's Special Pizza

This is the pizza that put us on the map. It has always been, and still is our number one seller. You can buy roasted red peppers in a jar at the market. But if you want to have the best flavor, roast them yourself. Its not difficult or even all that time consuming. We have the procedure on page 76.

Toppings (in order of assembly):

pizza sauce

mozzarella cheese

pepperoni

Italian sausage - preferably spicy

onions - slivered

mushrooms--sliced

roasted red peppers (if you want to roast your own, see procedure page 76)

Wines for pairing:

Suggested Wine with Gourmet Vegetarian: *Dolcetto d'Alba*

If you were to live in Piedmont, home of the huge Barolo and Barbaresco wines, you would more likely drink Dolcetto on a daily basis. Dolcetto, which means "little sweet one", is not a sweet wine though; but it can be quite fruity. It has more tannins and less acidity than Barbera. It is often drunk as a first course red wine with antipasti.

Frankie's recommendation: *Giribaldi Dolcetto d'Alba*

Suggested Wine with Mediterranean Pizza: *Rosato (Italian rosé)*

I'd never thought of pairing Rosato with pizza until we did our pairing sessions, and for two of the pizzas it turned out to be the best wine. The Gabbiano Rosato Toscana, made from Sangiovese grapes, has a nice pink strawberry color. The nose is fruity. On the palate, rich red fruits, medium mouth feel and a persistent finish..

Frankie's recommendation: *Gabbiano Rosato Toscana*

Suggested Wine with Frankie's Special: *Aglianico*

I love this wine from Campania so much that I've run it as a wine-of-the-month multiple times. Aglianico is considered one of the three noble grape varieties of Italy. It can make a huge wine, but for pizza or pasta I prefer a younger-drinking version like this one. The wine is still dry but with lovely fruit.

Frankie's recommendation: *Feudi di San Gregorio "Rubrato"*

The Vesuvius

The Vesuvius pizza is named for that famous volcano that buried Pompeii. It is one of my personal favorites on the menu. Its easy to make your own pesto if you desire. The recipe is on page 110.

Toppings (in order of assembly):

basil pesto - brushed generously atop dough

mozzarella cheese - about 1-1/4 cup

fontina cheese - about 1/2 cup

ricotta cheese - about 1/2 cup dabbed here and there

prosciutto ham - very thinly sliced

roasted red peppers (if you want to roast your own, see procedure page 76)

Frankie's Tip: Unless you have a meat slicer, it is hard to slice Prosciutto as thin as you want it. So I suggest you buy it pre-sliced, or have your butcher slice it.

Chicken Gorgonzola

I love gorgonzola cheese. It is related to bleu cheese but is a little less piquant. It works really well with the chicken on this pizza. I also love to pair it with Italian sausage.

Photo courtesy of Doug Adams Photography

Toppings (in order of assembly):

basil pesto - brushed generously atop dough

mozzarella cheese - about 1-3/4 cup

cooked chicken (light or dark, your preference) - sliced thin

onions - slivered

red bell peppers - sliced thin

gorgonzola cheese - about 1/3 cup

Frankie's Tip: A little gorgonzola goes a long way, so just crumble a moderate amount atop the pizza.

Three Olive Pizza

This is a pizza we serve on our winter seasonal menu, when there are not many fresh vegetables available. If you like olives, you will love this pizza. We use calamata, Spanish and green olives. Feel free to substitute any type of olives.

Toppings (in order of assembly):

pizza sauce

mozzarella cheese

salami - sliced thin

onions - slivered

three or more types of olives of your choice - sliced or simply pitted

Wines for pairing:

Suggested Wine with The Vesuvius: *Montepulciano d'Abruzzo*

There is confusion because there is a town in Tuscany called Montepulciano; and wines from there also have the name Montepulciano in them (such as *Vino Nobile de Montepulciano,* made from *Sangiovese*). For this wine the name indicates the name of the grape, and Abruzzo is the region. They are typically exceptional values.

Frankie's recommendation: *Capestrano Montepulciano d'Abruzzo*

Suggested Wine with Chicken Gorgonzola: *Negroamaro*

I expected a white wine to go best with this pizza and was surprised at the wine we chose. Negroamaro is named for its grape, which is grown in Apulia, the heel of Italy's boot. It means "black-bitter" or "blackest of the black". But what really worked here was the pairing between the gorgonzola cheese and the wine.

Frankie's recommendation: *Liveli "Passamante" Salento Negroamaro*

Suggested Wine with Three Olive Pizza: *Rosato (Italian rosé)*

Who would of thought that a rosé wine would have worked with a meaty and salty pizza. But sometimes opposites attract and this one does the trick. This rosé comes from Piedmont, where it is made primarily from Nebbiolo. It is a bright, violet-scented rosé with exquisite red berry fruit on the palate and a delightful mineral character.

Frankie's recommendation: *Proprieta Sperino 2008 Rosa del Rosa*

Walla Walla Onion & Sausage Pizza

We feature this pizza on our summer menu. The onions are the star of the show so put lots on. If the Italians grew these onions, you can be certain they would be putting them on a pizza.

Toppings (in order of assembly):

pizza sauce

fresh spinach - layered atop sauce

mozzarella cheese

Italian sausage (preferably spicy)

pancetta (or bacon) - pre-cooked and chopped

lots of Walla Walla onions - sliced thick

fresh Italian parsley - chopped (added after baking)

Wild Mushroom & Sausage Pizza

When autumn rolls around, one of the things I begin to crave is mushrooms. And wild mushrooms are more flavorful than your everyday button mushroom. We use fresh wild mushrooms, but sometimes you can find dried wild mushrooms and they are nearly as good. Don't hesitate to use them. We also use some smoked mozzarella on this, which works really well with the mushrooms. Buon appetito!

Toppings (in order of assembly):

pizza sauce

mozzarella cheese - a cup or more

smoked mozzarella cheese - about 1 cup

onions - slivered

Italian sausage (preferably spicy)

wild mushrooms

fresh Italian parsley - chopped (added after baking)

Frankie's Tip: For more info on wild mushrooms, check out the notes on my Wild Mushroom sauce on pages 124-125.

Harvest Moon Pie

I'm convinced this is the most unique pizza on the planet. I dreamed it up one autumn evening while watching a concert in the park and seeing a huge Harvest Moon rise up behind the trees. It features many ingredients which I associate with autumn, fresh Washington apples, applewood smoked bacon, cheddar cheese and walnuts. This pizza has developed a cult following at Frankie's.

Toppings (in order of assembly):

creamy sun-dried tomato pesto (see page 112)

mozzarella cheese - about 1 cup

sharp cheddar cheese - about 1 cup

gorgonzola cheese - about 1/4 cup scattered

onions - slivered

lots of bacon (preferably applewood smoked) - pre-cooked and chopped

apples (Gala apples work well) - diced small

walnuts - toasted in a skillet and chopped - scattered abroad

fresh Italian parsley - chopped (added after baking)

Wines for pairing:

Suggested Wine with Walla Walla Onion Pizza: *Sangiovese*

You probably know that Sangiovese is the grape they use to make Chianti. But it is also used to make many other Tuscan wines, including the noble Brunello di Montalcino; as well as many wines from Emilia-Romagna and Umbria. Sangiovese is known for its cherry and herb flavors, high acidity, and firm tannins.

Frankie's recommendation: *Poggio alle Sugheri Sangiovese*

Suggested Wine with Wild Mushroom Pizza: *Teroldego*

Teroldego is a little known indigenous grape variety grown in steep valleys, surrounded by the Dolomite mountains, in the Trentino-Alto Adige region of northern Italy. It can produce a dark, robust, spicy and tannic red wine. If you are unable to find this wine, come and find me. A good alternative is a Moretti "La Rossa" Bira from Italy.

Frankie's recommendation: *Foradori "Teroldego" Rotaliano*

Suggested Wine with Harvest Moon Pie: *Sangiovese*

Sangiovese (pronounced san joe VAE sae), is the number one planted grape variety in all of Italy. Sangiovese adapts to its terrior, so there are dozens of clones grown throughout central Italy. Monte Antico is a very consistent producer of this wine. There was also a white wine which worked well with this pizza: Campagnolo Pinot Grigio.

Frankie's recommendation: *Monte Antico Rosso*

Pizza Florentine

The name Florentine has come to be used with Italian dishes which feature spinach, an ingredient the Florentine's use a lot of. I have a friend who loves this pizza so much he dreams about it. He always buys a large, which he claims is the size of a Buick, and he and his wife make two or three meals out of it.

Photo courtesy of Doug Adams Photography

Toppings (in order of assembly):

pizza sauce

fresh spinach - scattered atop the sauce

mozzarella cheese

ricotta cheese - dabbed here and there

pepperoni

Italian sausage - preferably spicy

onions - slivered

black olives - sliced

red bell peppers - sliced thin

Frankie's Tip: It is important that a good layer of spinach goes down underneath the cheese.

Pizza Calabrese

Calabria is the toe of Italy's boot, a region where many Italian-Americans came from. One food which the Calabrian's use a lot are spicy peppers. They're so good I decided to create a pizza around them. We buy Italian red cherry peppers in a jar. If you can't find them, try a spicy red pepper of your choice.

Toppings (in order of assembly):

pizza sauce

mozzarella cheese

provolone cheese (optional)

Italian sausage - preferably spicy

red cherry peppers--or other spicy red peppers--sliced thin

Frankie's Tip: Feel free to use all mozzarella or a blend of mozz and provolone; or even better yet some Buffalo milk mozzarella. If using jarred peppers, rinse before using.

Pesto & Goat Cheese Pizza

I feel this pizza has some french influence, since it's made with goat cheese. I even re-named it *Pizza Provence* once but sales dropped off so I changed it back. Call it what you want. It's delicious! The one in the photo was shot on our whole wheat dough. I'll put that recipe in a future cook book.

Toppings (in order of assembly):

basil pesto - brushed generously atop dough

mozzarella cheese--about 1-3/4 cup

goat cheese--1/4 to 1/2 cup (Montrachet or Chevre)

artichoke hearts - broken up

red onion - thinly slivered

sun-dried tomatoes (oil packed or re-hydrated)

Frankie's Tip: Goat cheese is strong so use sparingly unless you are a huge fan.

Wines for pairing:

Suggested Wine with Pizza Florentine: *Barbera d'Asti*

Barbera, a grape from Piedmont, is considered by many to be the penultimate pizza and pasta wine. It is naturally low in tannins and high in acidity, giving it a juicy character which matches well with tomato sauce dishes. Barberas from Asti, tend to have slightly less structure and body than those from neighboring Alba.

Frankie's recommendation: *Vietti Barbera d'Asti*

Suggested Wine with Pizza Calabrese: *Gaglioppo*

I bet few of you have heard of this wine (pronounced gah-LYOHP-poh), which comes from Calabria. We recently featured it with this pizza at a wine dinner and the pairing was perfect. The wine has good structure and rich, spicy flavors. This is will be a bit hard to find but you could order it through us.

Frankie's recommendation: *Statti Gaglioppo*

Suggested Wine with Pesto & Goat Cheese Pizza: *Barbaresco*

Barbaresco is made from the Nebbiolo grape in the region of Piedmont, and is normally a big, structured and expensive wine; too big for a pizza like this. So I would only buy a less expensive one like this, which is lighter in structure and less tannic. It paired very nicely with this pie.

Frankie's recommendation: *Pasquale "Pelissero" Barbaresco*

Passion Pizza of Verona

I first developed this pizza for Valentine's day about ten years ago. It was such a huge hit that I had to add it to the menu to prevent an uprising. Its name of course is related to the beautiful and romantic city of Verona in the Italian region of Veneto, which was the backdrop for Romeo and Juliet.

Toppings (in order of assembly):

pizza sauce

basil pesto--drizzled atop the pizza sauce

fresh spinach--scattered atop the sauce

mozzarella cheese--about 1-3/4 cup

gorgonzola cheese--about 1/3 cup

Italian sausage--preferably spicy

artichoke hearts--broken up

roasted red peppers (to roast your own, see procedure page 76)

toasted pine nuts--scattered abroad

Frankie's Tip: To toast pine nuts, place them in a pan over medium heat and stir until lightly browned.

Wines for pairing:

Suggested Wine with Passion Pizza of Verona: *Soave*

Soave is made primarily from a grape known as Garganega which some believe to be of Etruscan origins. It is grown on high pergolas, in the hills near the town of Soave, not far from Verona in the region of Veneto. This wine has a lively freshness and juicy character with a very nice and unmistakable mineral note.

Frankie's recommendation: *Suavia Soave Classico*

Suggested Wine with Quattro Stagione: *Italian Syrah*

It's impossible to have one wine to match all seasons of this pizza. So I chose a wine I thought would work best. Syrah is one of the international grape varieties grown widely in Italy. One area it does well in is near the town of Cortona, made famous by Francis Mayes in her book *Under the Tuscan Sun*. I like this wine!

Frankie's recommendation: *La Braccesca "Achelo" Syrah*

Cast Iron "Quattro Stagione" Pizza

I wanted to bring my own style to this traditional Italian pizza meaning "four seasons"; which is divided into four quarters, for each season of the year. First, I did it deep dish-style in a cast iron skillet (you could do any pizza this way). Secondly, I modified the toppings. The most common toppings are mushrooms, olives, ham and artichoke hearts. Mine has prosciutto wrapped asparagus for spring, tomatoes and fresh basil for summer, wild mushrooms for the fall, and salami and olives for the winter. Feel free to vary with your favorite seasonal ingredients.

Toppings (in order of assembly):

pizza sauce

mozzarella cheese

fresh asparagus--hard end removed

prosciutto--sliced very thin

tomatoes--diced

fresh basil-torn

mushrooms--preferably wild--cut up

salami--diced

calamata olives

1. Preheat oven to 450º F. Liberally oil cast iron skillet (or other deep dish pan) with olive oil.

2. You'll need one normal size pizza dough plus a couple of ounces to make the cross pieces if desired (not all Quattro Stagione use this method). Press the dough into the skillet and up the sides.

3. Top with sauce and cheese. Roll out extra dough and place crisscross atop cheese.

4. Wrap asparagus with prosciutto. Place on 1/4. Moving clockwise, place tomatoes on next section, mushrooms on the next and finishing with the salami and olives. Wait to add basil until after baking.

5. Bake 15 to 18 minutes until well browned and crust is firm.

alzones

A calzone is a little like pizza except that the dough is folded over like a turnover to enclose the fillings. In Italy, calzones are generally made with mozzarella cheese, though they sometimes have provolone and parmesan. In America, it's become traditional to add ricotta cheese as well. The cheese mixture we use is shown below. Feel free to change it to your liking. Another tradition with calzones is to serve the sauce on the side. You can use either pizza sauce or marinara.

On page 96 you will see a step-by-step procedure on how to make calzones. However the filling ingredients are not listed there. We have shown some of our most popular calzones here.

Calzone Cheese Mixture (enough for two calzones):

3/4 cup ricotta cheese

1/2 cup mozzarella cheese

1 teaspoon dried basil

1 teaspoon dried oregano

Place in a bowl and mix well (you can use a mixer but fingers work even better).

House Special Calzone

Fillings (quantity per calzone):

calzone cheese mixture--about 2/3 cup

salami--3-4 slices

Italian Sausage (pre-cooked)--about 1/4 cup

onions--sliced

mushrooms--sliced

green bell peppers--sliced

1/2 cup pizza sauce--served on the side

Suggested Wine with House Special Calzone: *Nero d'Avola*

Nero d'Avola is a very dark skinned grape (Nero means black), named for the Avola region in southern Sicily; though the grape is actually native to Calabria where it is known as Calabrese. It is explosive with sun-baked Mediterranean flavors, with sweet tannins and peppery plum on the palate. A superb value!

Recommended Wine: *Regaleali Nero d'Avola*

Vegetarian Calzone

Fillings (quantity per calzone):

calzone cheese mixture--about 2/3 cup

fresh spinach--chopped

red onions--sliced

mushrooms--sliced

red bell peppers--sliced

tomatoes--sliced or chopped

1/2 cup pizza sauce--served on the side

Suggested Wine with Vegetarian Calzone: *Barbera d'Asti*

Barbera is one of my favorite everyday reds. This one from Carlin de Paolo recently won 1st place in the annual wine competition organized by the Chamber of Commerce, Industry, Craftsmanship and Agriculture of Asti. The wine has an intense aroma with prevailing flavors of cherry, liquorice, plum, violet, blackberries.

Recommended wine: *Carlin de Paolo Barbera d'Asti*

Calzone Veneto

Fillings (quantity per calzone):

calzone cheese mixture--about 2/3 cup

1/2 grilled chicken breast--cut in bite size pieces

prosciutto--thinly sliced and torn

fresh garlic--chopped

fresh spinach--chopped

onions--sliced

red bell peppers--sliced

a drizzle of fresh basil pesto

Suggested Wine with Calzone Veneto: *Dolcetto d'Alba*

Dolcetto (pronounced dohl CHET toh), is prized in its native Piedmont, not just for its deep color and spicy berry flavors, but because it ripens earlier than the other red varieties grown there. It is also an earlier maturing wine and is often served with the multiple antipasti courses typical of a Piemontese meal.

Recommended wine: *Ronchi Dolcetto d'Alba*

How to Make a Calzone:

Making a calzone has a lot in common with making a pizza. In one respect it is easier, because you roll out the dough instead of stretching it. One pizza dough will make 2 to 3 calzones, depending on how big you make them. This procedure below is for making two at once.

Pizza Stone Method (highly recommended!):

1. Prepare pizza dough and sauce according to recipes.

2. At least 45 minutes prior to baking, place pizza stone on middle rack of oven (with no racks above it) and pre-heat to 450° F.

3. Remove dough from refrigerator and allow to come to room temperature (20 to 30 minutes).

4. Sprinkle cornmeal or semolina flour on the wooden pizza peel. Sprinkle flour on work counter for rolling pizza dough. Place your dough on the floured surface. Lightly flour the dough and flour your hands as well.

5. Roll out the dough into a large oval using a rolling pin. If the dough becomes hard to roll out, set it aside and allow to rest for a few minutes. This will relax the glutens and make it more pliable.

6. Place two balls (about 2/3 cup each) of calzone cheese mixture (see recipes), on top of the dough about 5 to 6 inches apart (see photo). Press down to flatten out a bit. Add other toppings of your choice on top of the cheese (leave at least two inches between the piles of toppings).

7. Fold the dough over the top of the fillings. Use a pizza cutter to cut down the middle between the two calzones. Then cut around the filled portion to remove the excess dough. You want to attain two half-moon shapes with approximately an inch of dough around the toppings.

8. Use your fingers to roll the dough tightly around the edges. Then using a fork or a knife, poke holes in the top to allow steam to escape while baking.

9. Place the calzones, one at a time, on the wooden pizza peel. Shake the handle to make sure it is not sticking to the board (if it is, you need more cornmeal or semolina flour). Then, using the pizza peel, transfer the calzone to your pre-heated pizza stone. Repeat with second calzone, being careful that they do not touch in the oven.

10. Bake until the crust is brown and firm on the edges (about 12 to 15 minutes).

11. Use pizza peel to remove calzones. Brush crust lightly with olive oil, and sprinkle on some dried Italian herbs (if desired). Serve with a small bowl of warm pizza sauce on the side.

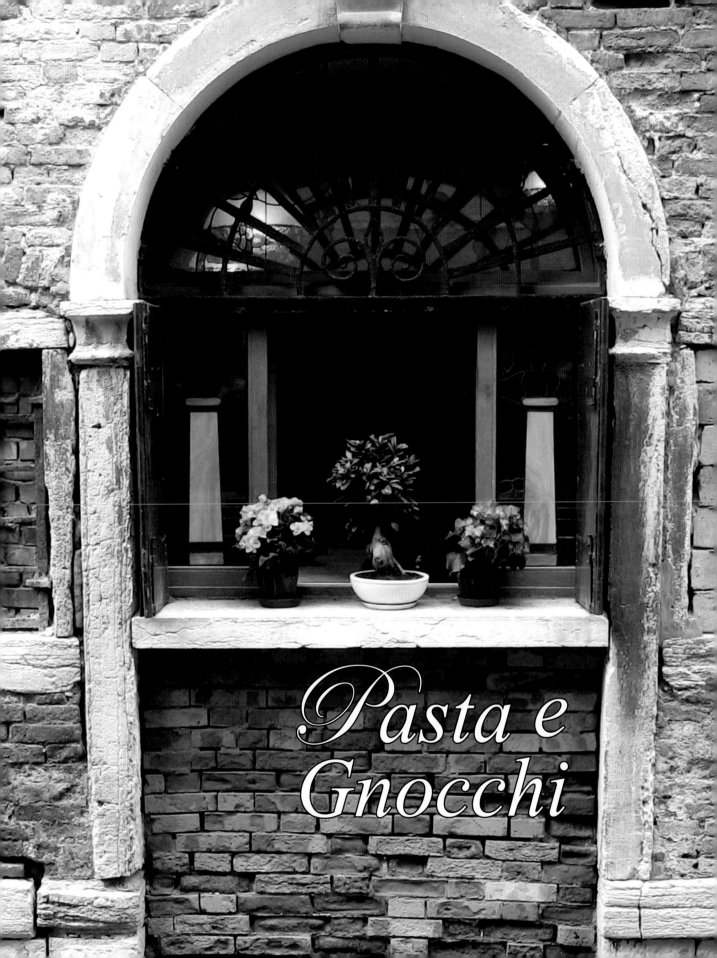

Pasta e
Gnocchi

Marinara Sauce

A good tomato sauce is delicious by itself, and also forms the base from which many delightful variations can be created. It is quick and easy to make. Many people do not want to bother making their own because they think the sauce needs to cook for hours. On the contrary, if you cook it for hours you lose the bright, zesty tomato flavors.

There are just a few simple keys to making a great sauce. First is to use high quality tomatoes. Good quality canned tomatoes are fine. Actually they are preferred by many chefs. Once a year or so, I like to make a sauce from fresh tomatoes when they are in peak season. The remainder of the time I use canned Italian Tomatoes.

In preparing for this cookbook, we tested sixteen brands of Crushed Tomatoes. We were looking for the optimum quality so the recipes in this book would be as good as we prepare in the restaurant. Please see page 15 for our recommendations.

8 servings

2 tablespoons olive oil

1 small (or 1/2 large) onion—finely chopped

3-4 cloves fresh garlic—pressed or minced

2 - 28 oz. cans Crushed Tomatoes

1/2 teaspoon dried oregano

1 teaspoon fresh Italian Parsley— chopped (or 1/2 teaspoon dried)

1 tablespoon fresh Basil—kissed by the sun—-julienned

1/2 teaspoon salt (preferably sea salt)

1/2 teaspoon sugar (or more to your taste)

1 tablespoon tomato paste

drizzle extra virgin olive oil

1. Mise en Place—prepare and measure out all ingredients in advance.

2. Drizzle Pure Olive Oil in a large, straight sided skillet (or sauce pan—3 qt. or larger), and heat over medium heat until oil begins to shimmer. Sauté onion until translucent. Add garlic and sauté for 1 to 2 additional minutes (do not burn the garlic!).

3. Add Crushed Tomatoes. Add herbs, salt, sugar and tomato paste. Check seasoning and adjust to your taste. Reduce heat to a simmer. Drizzle with extra virgin olive oil and stir in.

4. Unless you are preparing the sauce in advance, heat water for pasta; 3-4 quarts with teaspoon of salt in a large pot. Bring to a boil.

5. Cook 1-1/2 pounds pasta of your choice until al dente.

6. Drain pasta. Do not rinse. Toss with sauce and serve with grated parmesan Cheese. I highly recommend Parmigiano-Reggiano!

Suggested Wine: *Valpolicella*

In Veneto, they produce a wine called Valpolicella, made from the little known indigenous grapes Corvina, Rondinella, and Molinara. The wine is generally light-bodied, velvety, and very aromatic with soft tannins. It has flavors of cherry or berry fruits and a good acidity and zestiness which goes perfectly with Marinara.

Frankie's recommendation: *Allegrini Valpolicella Classico*

Frankie's Tips:

♦ You could easily cut this recipe in half, if you are cooking for a small crowd. But since the sauce freezes so well, I recommend you make the full recipe and freeze the remaining sauce for another meal.

♦ If you don't want to work with fresh garlic cloves, feel free to substitute minced garlic which comes in a jar. Substitute 1/2 teaspoon for each clove.

♦ For the best quality sauce, check out my canned tomato recommendations on page 15.

♦ This recipe calls for Crushed Tomatoes. If you like your sauce to have a chunkier consistency, use one can of Crushed and one can of Whole Peeled Tomatoes. You will have to break up the whole tomatoes, and cook it a little longer (or add additional tomato paste) to compensate for the additional liquid.

♦ Many people like to add wine to their tomato sauces. If you do, I recommend white wine, which will give you a brighter flavor and color. I would suggest 1/4 cup added just before the tomatoes.

Sicilian Meat Sauce

We call this sauce "Sicilian" because it is made with spicy Italian Sausage, unlike most meat sauces which are made with ground beef. Otherwise it is pretty similar to a traditional meat sauce; or ragu as the Italians would call it.

8 servings

2 tablespoons olive oil

1 small (or 1/2 large) onion—chopped

3-4 ounces fresh button mushrooms— sliced or quartered

3-4 cloves fresh garlic—minced

1-1/2 pounds Italian sausage (I prefer spicy)

1/4 cup white wine

2 - 28 oz. cans Crushed Tomatoes

1 teaspoon dried oregano (or 1 tablespoon fresh)

1 teaspoon fresh Italian parsley— chopped (or 1/2 teaspoon dried)

1+ tablespoon fresh basil—julienned

3/4 teaspoon salt (preferably sea salt)

1/2 teaspoon sugar (or more to your taste)

1 tablespoon tomato paste

drizzle extra virgin olive oil

1. Put on some Italian music and pour a glass of wine.
2. Mise en Place—prepare and measure out onions, mushrooms, garlic and fresh herbs. Measure out salt, sugar, and dried herbs. Open tomatoes. If sausage is in links, remove from casing.
3. Drizzle olive oil in a large, straight sided skillet (or sauce pan—3 qt. or larger), and heat over medium heat until oil begins to shimmer. Add onion and sauté for about one minute. Add mushrooms and sauté until tender, about 3-4 minutes.
4. Add sausage. Chop and stir with a wooden spatula until most of the pink is gone. Add garlic and sauté 1-2 minutes more.
5. Add wine to deglaze. Scrape and stir for 1-2 minutes until wine partially evaporates. Add oregano, sauté briefly.
6. Add Crushed Tomatoes, herbs, salt, sugar and tomato paste. Check seasoning and adjust to your taste. Reduce heat to a simmer. Drizzle with extra virgin olive oil and stir in.
7. Unless you are preparing the sauce in advance, heat water for pasta; 3-4 quarts water with teaspoon of salt in a large pot. Bring to a boil.
8. Cook 1-1/2 pounds of your favorite pasta until al dente.
9. Drain pasta. Do not rinse. Toss with sauce and serve with freshly grated cheese. I recommend Parmigiano-Reggiano or a good quality Pecorino Romano.

Frankie's Tips:

♦ Feel free to substitute spicy Chicken Italian Sausage for pork sausage. I like it equally as well and of course it is leaner--which will help you stay leaner.

♦ Once again, let me say that using high quality canned tomatoes is a must. See page 15 for my recommendations.

♦ Sugar is a very subjective thing with tomato sauces. I dislike most commercial sauces because they use way too much for my taste. I prefer just a light touch. Feel free to leave it out or add more to your taste.

Suggested Wine: *Nero d'Avola*

A Sicilian sauce calls for a Sicilian wine, and Nero d'Avola is Sicily's most prominent red wine, and one which goes perfectly with this sauce.

Nero d'Avola is a very dark skinned grape (Nero meaning black) and named for the Avola region in southern Sicily. It is explosive with sun-baked Mediterranean flavors, with sweet tannins and peppery plum on the palate.

Frankie's recommendation: *Colosi Nero d'Avola*

Spaghetti with Meat Balls

Who doesn't love spaghetti and meatballs? I'd venture to say that some vegetarians have dreams about them. But for a week or two, my wife did not want to see another meatball! This was because I made dozens and dozens of them trying to get this recipe perfect. We had spaghetti with meatballs, meatball sandwiches, meatballs in the refrigerator, meatballs in the freezer, we fed them to family visiting for the holidays. But all of this hard work paid off. I believe this is one of the best meatballs you are ever going to eat, maybe even better than your Italian Nana makes (but don't tell her—you might hurt her feelings—or she might have your cousin Guido come after me).

I like my meatballs baked, though you may pan fry them in oil if you prefer, which will yield a darker, crustier exterior. A mini muffin pan is ideal for baking; providing for even cooking. If you do not have one, you can bake them on a sheet pan. Buon appetito!

4-6 servings

Meatball Ingredients:

2 slices of white bread—crusts removed—torn into pieces

3 ounces buttermilk

3/4 pound ground chuck—chilled (see Frankie's Tips)

1/4 pound ground pork—chilled

1/3 cup finely grated Parmesan Cheese

2 tablespoons fresh Italian parsley—minced

1 large egg yolk

2 cloves—finely minced garlic

3/4 teaspoon salt

ground black pepper—several twists

Pasta Ingredients:

1/2 recipe Frankie's Marinara Sauce

1 pound spaghetti

Preparing the Meatballs:

1. Combine the crust-less bread and buttermilk in a shallow bowl. Allow to soak for 10 minutes, mashing occasionally with a fork until it forms a smooth paste.

2. Preheat oven to 400° F.

3. Spray mini muffin tin with non-stick cooking spray (preferably olive oil or canola). Note—if using a baking pan you can either spray the pan with non-stick cooking spray or use a Silpat baking mat.

4. Place all remaining meatball ingredients in a medium mixing bowl. Add the bread-buttermilk mixture and combine with your hands until well incorporated.

5. This recipe should yield 12 or more meatballs, depending on how big you want them. Divide the meat in four sections, and then divide each section by three (alternatively you can weigh them out at 1.75 ounces each).

6. Use the palms of your hands to shape the meatballs into rounds and place in individual muffin tin cups.

7. Bake meatballs for 18 minutes.

8. If using for spaghetti, place the meatballs in your sauce and cook an additional 4 to 5 minutes.

Preparing the Spaghetti:

1. Prepare Marinara Sauce per recipe.

2. When meatballs are nearing completion, cook pasta according to package directions.

3. Toss pasta with sauce and top with meatballs.

Suggested Wine: *Barbera*

Barbera, which comes from Piedmont, is considered by many to be the penultimate pizza and pasta wine. It is naturally low in tannins and high in acidity, giving it a juicy character which matches well with tomato sauce dishes. This version, designated as 'Superiore', gets a little more oak aging than a traditional Barbera; thus it has a little more body and structure.

Frankie's recommendation: *Carlin d'Paolo Barbera d'Asti Superiore*

Frankie's Tips:

♦ This recipe is easy to double. Meatballs freeze extremely well so that you can have them later for pasta or meatball sandwiches.

♦ Keep your meat chilled until ready to mix. Room temperature meat will be very mushy and the meatballs will not hold their shape well; besides which you run a higher risk of food borne illness. Also make certain meatballs are cooked to at least 160° F, as tested with a thermometer.

♦ When mixing the meat with other ingredients, do not mix anymore than necessary because that will make the meat tougher.

♦ I tried several combinations of meat and really liked the 3 to 1 ratio of ground beef to pork. I tried veal in the recipe but found the meatballs to be bland. Unless you go to a meat counter which has bulk ground meats, you'll likely have to buy a whole pound of ground pork. Save the extra for meatloaf or for making sausage.

♦ A great alternative is to substitute ground lamb instead of pork for a richer flavor. You can also make the meatballs from ground chicken if you want a healthier alternative. It tends to be softer, so refrigerate the mix for an hour before cooking. Also cook to 165° F.

Pomodoro Sauce

This delicious sauce is a lighter, fresher version of tomato sauce and is super quick and easy to make. It's not cooked, and I recommend minimal contact with heat when warming it. It is also delicious cold, so you could use it in a cold pasta salad or serve it chilled with angel hair or spaghetti on a hot summer day.

5-6 servings

1 - 28 oz. can Whole Peeled Tomatoes

2-3 cloves fresh garlic—pressed

1/4 cup fresh basil—julienned

1/2 teaspoon salt (preferably Sea Salt)

1/2 teaspoon sugar (or more to your taste)

1/4 cup extra virgin olive oil

1. Smell the fresh basil and say "thank you" to God for the good things in life.

2. Place the tomatoes with their juice in a large bowl. With your hands, crush and break up the tomatoes.

3. Stir in remaining ingredients. Refrigerate. I told you this was quick and easy!

Frankie's Tips:

♦ This sauce is at its best if made in advance so the flavors meld together. I suggest making it at least four hours before serving, or even a day ahead.

♦ For the best quality sauce, check out my canned tomato recommendations on page 15.

Angel Hair Pomodoro

This recipe features our Pomodoro Sauce which is a lighter, fresher version of Tomato Sauce. If you can make the sauce a day ahead it will taste even better, and you could have dinner ready in minutes. It can be made with any pasta but a thin pasta works very well. Buon appetito!

5~6 servings

1 pound angel hair pasta

1 recipe Pomodoro Sauce
(see recipe—previous page)

8 ounces fresh mozzarella

Italian parsley—chopped
(for garnish)

1. Prepare Pomodoro Sauce and set aside.

2. Heat 4 quarts of water and add a tablespoon of salt when it begins to boil.

3. Place fresh mozzarella on paper towels and roll around to drain excess liquid. Rough chop into 1/4 inch pieces.

4. When water is boiling, cook pasta until nearly "al dente" (about one minute less than package instructions). Drain pasta and return to pot.

5. Pour Pomodoro sauce over pasta and toss. Warm over low heat for about two minutes until pasta is "al dente".

6. Platter and top with chopped fresh mozzarella (see Frankie's Tip's below). Garnish with Italian parsley.

7. Raise a glass and make a toast to those whom God has given you to love (for a fun toast, see page 218).

Suggested Wine: *Nebbiolo*

Nebbiolo, which hails from the northern Italian region of Piedmont is the grape that is used for making the prominent wines, Barolo and Barbaresco. Those wines are way too big for a delicate dish like this. When aged less, as it is for this wine, it is lighter-bodied and works very well with this sauce.

Frankie's recommendation: *Damilano Nebbiolo d'Alba*

Frankie's Tips:

♦ Because angel hair is so thin it can overcook very easily and turn to mush. Therefore you want to under-cook it some before adding it in with the sauce where it will continue cooking. Check it frequently as it nears the latter cooking stages.

♦ For a while I made a change in this recipe at the restaurant, and began to add the fresh mozzarella into the pasta and sauce after it was tossed together; allowing the cheese to melt slightly. Personally I prefer it this way, but most of my customers liked the uncooked cheese on top, so we went back to preparing it that way. Either will work well.

♦ This dish is also delightful with sautéed shrimp in it!

Pasta Bolognese

I don't want to boast, but I spent much time fine-tuning this sauce, and I must say; that it is one of the best pasta sauces I have ever tasted. It was so good I almost wanted to cry!

This sauce originates from the proud city of Bologna (thus the name), which lies in the heart of the fertile Po Valley in Emilia-Romagna, in north-central Italy. It is a very cultured city which many consider to be the culinary capitol of Italy. If this sauce is any indication, I would agree.

Bolognese is different from other meat sauces in that the meat is the star of the show, with the tomatoes in a supporting role. But there is one catch, you must start this sauce early in the afternoon, because it needs more than an hour to prepare and another three hours to simmer very slowly. This tenderizes the meat so it melts in your mouth, causing your taste buds to scream bravo, bravo!

5-6 servings

1/4 cup butter

3/4 cup onion—chopped fine

1/2 cup carrot—chopped fine

1/2 cup celery—chopped fine

6 ounces Pancetta—diced in small pieces (1/4" or smaller)

1 clove garlic—minced

3/4 pound ground beef*

3/4 pound ground veal*

1/2 teaspoon salt

1 cup whole milk

1/2 cup chicken stock

1-1/4 cup dry white wine (such as Pinot Grigio)

1—28 oz. can Whole Peeled Tomatoes —broken up with your hands

3/4 cup canned Tomato Sauce

pinch crushed red peppers (optional)

fresh ground black pepper

1 pound hearty pasta—such as rigatoni (my favorite), fettuccine or tagliatelle

parmesan (preferably Parmigiano-Reggiano) - grated or curled

2 tablespoons Italian parsley—chopped

1. Heat the butter over medium heat in a heavy-bottomed Dutch oven or a large deep skillet. Sauté the onion, carrots and celery until softened, about 5 minutes.

2. Add Pancetta and sauté for 5 minutes. Add the garlic, and cook until onions begin to brown and garlic is softened and fragrant—2-3 minutes.

3. Add the ground meats and 1/2 teaspoon salt. As meat cooks, chop it relatively fine with the back of a wooden spoon, until it just loses its raw color, about 3 to 4 minutes.

4. Add the milk and simmer until it evaporates, about 10 to 12 minutes (there will still be some clear liquid visible from the fats).

5. Add the white wine and simmer until it evaporates, 12 to 15 minutes. Use your wooden spoon to scrape any browned-bits from the bottom of the pan (lot's of flavor!).

6. Add the Whole Peeled Tomatoes with their juices, the Tomato Sauce, the chicken stock, and a pinch of crushed red peppers if desired. Bring to a simmer. Then reduce heat as low as it will go and simmer, stirring occasionally, for 3 hours (see Frankie's Tip's).

7. Add several twists of fresh ground black pepper. Taste and adjust salt and pepper as needed.

8. When the sauce is almost done cooking, bring a large pot to a boil over high heat and add a tablespoon of salt. Cook your pasta until nearly al dente. Reserve about a 1/4 cup of pasta water before draining.

9. Drain pasta and return to the pasta pot. Stir the sauce into the pasta and pour in the reserved pasta water. Cook over medium heat for about 2 minutes, stirring constantly.

10. Serve up with parmesan and garnish with Italian parsley.

Suggested Wine: *Sangiovese*

You'd think after all the time making this sauce that it would call for a really exceptional wine, yet I found that an easy drinking Sangiovese worked best with it. Bigger wines competed with it's subtle flavors. A Sangiovese from Emilia-Romagne would be wonderful but hard to find. This moderately-priced Tuscan version worked just right.

Frankie's recommendation: *Primavera Sangiovese*

Frankie's Tips:

♦ The primary reason for the three hour simmer is to properly tenderize the meat. Shorter times will not accomplish this well. The sauce will still have great flavor, but not the desired texture. Cooking hotter for a shorter time also does not work well. Only a long, and very slow simmer will get the job done right.

♦ When simmering properly, the sauce should just have a few bubbles coming up through it. Cooking at too brisk of a simmer will evaporate too much liquid. However, many ranges do not cook at a low enough temperature. There is a very simple solution though...

♦ Using tin foil, pull off two sheets about 14 to 16 inches long each. Lay them atop one another, and then starting with the long side, roll them up into a long snake. Bend it in to a circle, joining the two ends so you have a ring. Place that on top of your burner and place the pan on top of the ring. This lifts the pan and creates some insulation which will slow the simmer.

♦ I strongly suggest that you stick with the whole milk in this recipe for the richness it provides. If you don't have any whole milk but happen to have some cream or half & half around, add a little to your lower fat milk to balance it out.

♦ The pancetta in this recipe is best if it is cubed, as opposed to sliced thin like bacon.

♦ If you desire to double the recipe I strongly suggest you use two separate pans.

Fresh Basil Pesto

Fresh Basil Pesto tastes like summer, and conjures up memories of our trip to Cinque Terre on the Ligurian coast of Italy, where this sauce originated (in nearby in Genova). This sauce has many uses: on pizza, pasta, fish, shrimp, chicken, or to dress vegetables. It is equally good warm or cold.

Pesto freezes well. I make a double recipe once or twice each summer, with basil I grow in my garden. I transfer the pesto to 4 ounce disposable food containers and pour a thin layer of olive oil over the top, which keeps it fresh and green (this can also be done with leftover pesto which you plan to store in the refrigerator). A single recipe will yield two containers.

6 servings

2 cups packed fresh basil leaves—stems removed

1 tablespoon fresh Italian parsley—chopped (optional)

1/4 cup walnuts or pine nuts—lightly toasted

2-3 cloves fresh Garlic—lightly toasted

1/4 teaspoon salt (preferably sea salt)

1/2 cup extra virgin olive oil

1/2 cup finely grated Parmigiano-Reggiano

2 tablespoon softened butter (optional)

1 teaspoon fresh squeezed Lemon Juice (optional)

1. If using walnuts, chop roughly. Toast nuts in a dry, heavy duty skillet over medium heat, stirring frequently until golden and fragrant, about 4-5 minutes. Set aside.

2. Place garlic cloves (skin on) in the same skillet. Toast, shaking the pan periodically, until they darken slightly in color and become fragrant, about 5 minutes. Transfer to a cutting board to cool, skin and chop roughly.

3. De-stem, rinse and dry fresh basil using a salad spinner or paper towels. Place the basil, parsley, nuts, garlic, salt and olive oil in food processor. Process until semi-smooth. You'll need to stop the processor once or twice to scrape down the bowl.

4. Transfer the pesto to a bowl. Stir in the grated cheese and butter and lemon juice if using. Taste and adjust salt if needed. If freezing, transfer to small containers and top with a thin layer of oil. It can also be refrigerated for 3-4 days. Place in a food storage container and cover with a thin layer of oil.

Fresh Basil:

Obviously you want the freshest basil possible! If you don't want to grow your own, one option is to purchase a live plant from your local farmer's market (they often carry them at Trader Joe's as well). Most supermarkets carry fresh basil. You'll need at least four ounces to provide the 2 cups of leaves you need for a single recipe.

Frankie's Tips:

♦ Be sure to remove the stems from the basil, especially the larger ones. If left in your pesto it will be very stringy.

♦ The Parsley is not critical but I like the flavor dimension it brings. It also brightens the color.

♦ If you are willing to take a couple of extra steps, they will make your pesto that little bit better. The first is to toast the nuts in a dry skillet, which will enhance their flavor. The other is to toast the garlic as well, which will tame the harshness which raw garlic can bring.

♦ Adding butter is a tip I learned from Marcella Hazan's cook book, Essentials of Classic Italian Cooking. I've made it with and without and like both. The butter adds a touch of creaminess and richness.

♦ The optional lemon juice is something one of my chef's came up with. I like the freshness it adds to the flavor. Its acidity will also help the pesto maintain its bright green color.

♦ Heat is the enemy of pesto! When using for pasta, do not heat pesto in a pan or it will separate and become bitter. Simply toss it with the warm pasta and an ounce or two of hot pasta water.

♦ Walnuts vs pine nuts. Pine nuts are traditional and will give you the smoothest, creamiest pesto, but they are very expensive. Walnuts are an excellent substitute, but make sure your guests are not allergic. I've even used pecans and was happy with the results.

Sun-dried Tomato Pesto

We've served this pesto at the restaurant ever since we opened. It is very popular. We serve it in our *Penne with Sun-dried Tomato Pesto* and on our *Mediterranean Pizza*. My favorite way to have it though is blended with cream sauce to create our *Creamy Sun-dried Tomato Pesto*, which we serve with a *Sun-dried Tomato Ravioli*. It is very versatile, and freezes well, so I have made the recipe large enough that you'll have extra to freeze for future uses, or to use in variations.

Yields about 3 cups—enough for 2 or more pounds of pasta

1/4 cup fresh basil—roughly chopped

2-3 garlic cloves—roughly chopped

1/4 cup walnuts (or pine nuts)

1 teaspoon salt

1/2 teaspoon chili powder

1/4 teaspoon balsamic vinegar

1/2 teaspoon red wine (optional)

1/2 teaspoon paprika (optional)

1 teaspoon Italian parsley

1/2 cup onion—roughly chopped

1/2 cup grated parmesan cheese (preferably Parmigiano-Reggiano)

5 ounces (2 cups) sun-dried tomatoes—see note below

1-1/4 cup olive oil—see Frankie's Tips

1. Rehydrate dried tomatoes in hot water. 5 ounces of dried tomatoes will yield about 2 cups. To rehydrate, soak in hot water for 30 to 40 minute (or boiling water for 20 minutes if you want to speed the process). Drain thoroughly and pat dry before using.

2. Place all ingredients—except for the sun-dried tomatoes and oil—in the bowl of a food processor. Process for 5 to 10 seconds or until finely chopped. Scrape bowl and process a few seconds more.

3. Add sun-dried tomatoes. Turn on processor and begin to add oil slowly through feed tube until fully incorporated and tomatoes are finely chopped.

4. Remove lid and scrape down sides of bowl. Process a few seconds more.

Frankie's Tips:

♦ Extra virgin olive oil is always ideal from a flavor standpoint but is expensive. I used 1/4 cup of EVOO and the remainder of pure olive oil. You could also blend EVOO with canola oil.

♦ For pasta, use just enough to coat the pasta well—about 2 ounces per person or 1-1/4 cups per pound of pasta. Whatever you don't use at this time can be frozen. I generally freeze pesto in small 4 ounce plastic storage containers which is enough for my wife and I to have for a quick and easy pasta dinner.

Regarding Sun-dried Tomatoes: This recipe uses the dried version of sun-dried tomatoes—as opposed to the oil packed version found in jars. In our local market the dried version are found in the produce section. If you can't find them, ask around. They are much more economical, and yield better results.

If substituting the oil packed version—reduce the quantity to 1-3/4 cups, which means you'll likely need to purchase two small jars (the store brands I found ranged from 6.5 to 8.5 ounces).

Sun-dried Tomato Pesto variations:

Creamy Sun-dried Tomato Pesto: This is delicious! Comfort food at its finest. But a few more calories of course. The ratio I like on this is about two parts cream sauce to one part SDT pesto. You can either use Alfredo sauce which you have prepared, or place one pint of Heavy Cream in a skillet and reduce by approximately one quarter—until slightly thickened—but still a nice creamy color. Add 6 ounces (3/4 cup) of Sun-dried Tomato Pesto and stir together. This will yield about 18 ounces—enough for a pound of pasta.

Spicy Red Passion Pesto: This spicier version of pesto is wonderful on any pasta. My wife and I enjoyed it with bow-tie pasta with some Italian Sausage added; bene, bene, molto bene! We have served it as a special at Frankie's with Black Bean Ravioli which was fabuloso!

To make this variation, cut a red bell pepper in quarters, brush with olive oil and roast under your broiler until the skin is blackened—about 20 to 25 minutes. Place in a plastic container and cover. Allow to cool until cool enough to handle. Remove the blacked skin. Place 1 cup of the Sun-dried Tomato pesto into your food processor with the roasted pepper and add 2 teaspoons of hot chili sauce (such as Frank's Red Hot Chili Sauce) and 3/4 teaspoon of crushed red pepper flakes. Process briefly. Adjust spices to taste.

Pasta with Sun-dried Tomato or Basil Pesto

At Frankie's, we serve penne rigate pasta with a choice of of either Sun-dried Tomato Pesto or Basil-Walnut Pesto. We also offer both pastas with the addition of Chicken or Shrimp. I highly recommend making some of both pestos and placing them in small containers in the freezer. If you've done so, you can have this on the table in about 20 minutes!

Serves 5-6

1 pound pasta--I recommend either penne rigate or linguine

1/4 cup pine nuts

1-2 tablespoon olive oil

1/2 cup calamata olives--pitted and roughly chopped

1/4 cup sun-dried tomatoes

7-8 artichoke hearts--broken up

1-1/4 cup of either Basil Pesto or Sun-dried Tomato Pesto

freshly grated parmesan cheese--for garnish (Parmigiano-Reggiano is best)

chopped Italian parsley--optional for garnish

1 pound shrimp or sliced chicken--optional

1. Prepare pesto sauce and set aside. This can be done a day or two ahead (or even farther ahead and frozen).
2. Begin water for pasta—3-4 quarts with a tablespoon of salt added after the water begins to boil.
3. Toast pine nuts in a large, dry sauté pan over medium heat. Stir regularly until light to medium brown.
4. Add olive oil to pan with pine nuts. If adding optional shrimp or chicken, add now. Sauté until nearly fully cooked; then add the olives, sun-dried tomatoes and artichoke hearts and sauté another minute or so. Turn heat to lowest setting, and then stir in pesto sauce.
5. Start your pasta while vegetables are sautéing. Cook pasta to al dente. Reserve about a quarter cup of the pasta water before draining pasta.
6. Combine cooked pasta with pesto and other ingredients and toss well. Garnish with grated parmesan and parsley.

Frankie's Tips:

♦ I really only have one tip here, and that is not to apply too much heat to the pesto. This will cause it to break down and separate.

Suggested Wine with Sun-dried Tomato Pesto: *Sicilia Rosso*

This little gem from Sicily is made from four Sicilian grapes, Nero d'Avola, Nerello Mascalese, Frappato and Nerello Cappuccio. It is very affordable and a great match with this dish.

Frankie's recommendation: *Dievole "Fourplay" Sicilia Rosso*

Suggested Wine with Basil Pesto: *Foja Tonda*

Of all the wines listed in my cook book, this red from the far northern reaches of Veneto is the most obscure. We tasted a lot of wines with the basil pesto though, and this one was clearly the best match. So I chose to put it in the book, even knowing it will be difficult to find. But hey, you can always order some through me!

Frankie's recommendation: *Albino Armani "Casetta" Foja Tonda*

Garlic Cream Sauce - aka Alfredo Sauce

One great thing about this sauce is that you can make so many delightful variations from it.

The original recipe, developed in a restaurant in Rome called "Alfredo's" —uses only butter and parmesan cheese. We make our Alfredo sauce the way it has become traditional to do so in America, with heavy cream. Many people use a combination of cream and butter, but we have found that by using heavy cream, which is high in butterfat, the butter is not needed at all (we only use it here to sauté the garlic). Therefore it would be more accurate to call this a Garlic Cream Sauce.

Yields about 3 cups—enough for one pound of pasta which will serve 5-6

1 teaspoon butter

3-4 cloves fresh garlic— minced (optional)

1 quart heavy cream

1/2 teaspoon garlic powder (optional)

fresh ground black pepper

1/2 teaspoon salt

1 cup freshly grated parmesan cheese (preferably Parmigiano-Reggiano) plus additional for garnishing pasta

2 tablespoons Italian parsley—chopped

1. Melt butter in a large skillet over low-medium heat.
2. Sauté garlic, stirring often, until softened and fragrant— about 2-3 minutes.
3. Stir in heavy cream, garlic powder, salt and several twists of black (or white) pepper.
4. Simmer over low heat until reduced to by about 1/4 (the sauce should easily coat back of a spoon) — about 12 to 15 minutes. Taste and adjust seasonings.
5. If serving immediately, start water for pasta in a large pot as soon as sauce begins to simmer. By the time the pasta is cooked the sauce should be ready (if not, drain the pasta and set aside briefly).
6. When the sauce is reduced enough, add the pasta, along with the grated parmesan, and toss well.
7. Transfer to serving dish. Grate additional fresh parmesan over the top and garnish with parsley.
8. If not using right away, place is a shallow dish—cool completely before covering. Refrigerate (up to three days). Re-warm slowly before using.

Suggested Wine: *Italian Chardonnay*

Generally speaking, Italian Chardonnays have less oak than new world Chardonnay's and therefore lack buttery character. However, it's best to have a little butteriness to match this dish, so if you are not able to find the Chardonnay listed, inquire after one which has some oak aging.

Frankie's recommendation: *Nozzole "LeBruniche" Chardonnay Toscana*

Frankie's Tips:

♦ I highly recommend that you use *heavy cream* for this as opposed to whipping cream, which is lighter in butter-fat. Whipping cream has to be cooked down much more to achieve a good consistency, and thus will yield about a third less of the finished sauce.

♦ Keep your heat fairly low when cooking this. Too much heat can cause the sauce to separate and will also turn it a light brown color, as opposed to a creamy white.

Smoked Salmon Pasta
With a White Wine, Lemon and Cream Sauce

This sauce is a simple variation of our Garlic Cream Sauce. One of the best things about living in the northwest is the abundance of salmon. I like to use ocean-caught salmon, as opposed to farmed Atlantic salmon which I believe is inferior. When we make this at the restaurant we use an alderwood smoked salmon which is perfect.

Serves 5~6

1 pound pasta (I prefer sea shell or bow-tie pasta)

2 tablespoons olive oil

1 pound smoked salmon--broken into bite size pieces

1 batch White Wine, Lemon and Cream Sauce (see Cream Sauce recipe and variations on pages 116 and 119)

fresh chives--cut in long pieces, enough for garnish

1. Prepare White Wine, Lemon and Cream Sauce and set aside. This can be done a day ahead if you like.

2. Begin water for pasta—3-4 quarts with a tablespoon of salt added after the water begins to boil. Cook pasta to al dente.

3. While pasta is cooking, heat olive oil in a large sauté pan or straight sided skillet over medium heat. Add salmon and sauté briefly until warmed through. Add sauce and re-warm slowly over low heat.

4. Drain pasta and add to salmon and sauce mixture. Toss well.

5. Platter and garnish with fresh chives.

Rigatoni Pasta with Shrimp and Prosciutto
With Red Bell Pepper Cream Sauce

This pasta, which is my own creation, just might be my favorite pasta in the world. I only eat it occasionally though, because as you know, cream sauces are not great for the waistline. The sautéed peppers give this sauce a beautiful, rich pink color. The sauce can be made a day ahead if you desire.

Serves 5-6

1 pound rigatoni pasta

2 tablespoons olive oil

1 small red bell pepper--cored, seeded, and sliced 1/4 inch thick or less

12 ounces of shrimp--peeled and deveined--tails off

1 ounce of prosciuttto--sliced paper thin--torn into pieces

1 batch Garlic Cream Sauce (see recipe page 116) made without the addition of parmesan cheese

1. Prepare Garlic Cream sauce (without parmesan cheese), and set aside. This can be done a day ahead if you like.

2. Begin water for pasta—3-4 quarts with a tablespoon of salt added after the water begins to boil.

3. Heat olive oil in a large sauté pan or straight sided skillet over medium heat. Add sliced red bell peppers and sauté until they soften and begin to give off some color to the oil.

4. Add shrimp and sauté until they are opaque and have a nice white-coral color, but are still moist. Add prosciutto when shrimp are nearly cooked and sauté briefly. Add sauce and re-warm slowly over low heat.

5. Cook pasta to al dente. Drain and add to shrimp and sauce mixture. Toss well.

6. Platter and garnish with a sprig of fresh basil or parsley.

Suggested Wine: *Soave*

Soave is made in the region of Veneto primarily from a grape known as Garganega. Its name, as you may have guessed, means "suave", which describes its character. At its best, it is a fruity, dry, fresh, straw-colored wine with style and elegance. Pieropan is one of my favorite producers.

Frankie's recommendation:
Pieropan Soave Classico

Sorrento, Campania

*M*ore Cream Sauce variations:

On the recipe variations for Sun-dried Tomato Pesto you will see a variation for *Creamy Sun-dried Tomato Pesto,* just one of many yummy variations you can do with this sauce!

When blending sauces, the ratio of one sauce to the other is really a matter of taste, and can range from three parts cream sauce to one part other--or the reverse--depending on how rich and creamy you want to make the sauce.

Creamy Tomato Sauce (aka - Pink Sauce or Aurora Sauce): This is made by blending Cream Sauce with either Marinara or Pomodoro sauce. The marinara will be slightly richer; the Pomodoro will create a sauce which is little chunkier and lighter in style. I like about a ratio of about two parts tomato sauce to one part cream, or maybe a touch less on the Cream Sauce. I really like these sauce blends with baked pastas. We serve a creamy Pomodoro with our Roasted Vegetable Manicotti (recipe page 138).

Creamy Basil Pesto: We often serve a special at the restaurant made with Cheese Tortellini and this sauce. You can either use Alfredo sauce which you have prepared, or place one pint of Heavy Cream in a skillet and reduce by approximately one quarter—until slightly thickened—but still a nice creamy color (no parmesan cheese should be added). Add 6 ounces (3/4 cup) of Basil Pesto and stir together. This will yield about 18 ounces—enough for a pound of pasta.

White Wine, Lemon and Cream Sauce: This variation is as easy as the others. To a full batch of Cream Sauce, add about 4 ounces of white wine and an 2 ounces of lemon juice. Adjust to taste. No parmesan cheese should be added to this recipe. This sauce is especially good on seafood pastas, or Pasta Primavera with grilled or sautéed vegetables!

 Penne Roma

With Chicken Italian Sausage, Olives & Onions in a creamy Tomato Sauce

This is one of my favorite dishes. It is real comfort food. The tomato sauce is made richer by the addition of a little cream. Feel free to substitute pork sausage if you like. I prefer it with spicy Chicken Italian Sausage.

5-6 servings

1 pound penne rigate pasta

12 ounces spicy Chicken Italian Sausage

2 tablespoons olive oil

3/4 cup black olives--sliced

1 cup slivered onions

1-2 cloves garlic

1 cup heavy cream

2-1/2 cups Marinara sauce

Parmigiano-Reggiano—fresh grated or shaved with vegetable peeler

Italian Parsley—chopped (for garnish)

1. Sliver onions and set aside. Chop garlic fine. Drain olives and slice if whole.

2. Heat one tablespoon olive oil in a large, straight-sided skillet over medium heat. Sauté Italian sausages until brown on exterior. Add water to cover sausages about half way, and continue to cook until slightly pink in center (they will continue to cook in sauce). Remove sausages and set aside. Drain water from pan and return to heat.

3. Add another tablespoon olive oil and sauté onions and olives for one minute. Add garlic and sauté an additional minute.

4. Add cream and reduce by approximately one quarter. Add Marinara and reduce heat to simmer.

5. Begin water for penne—3-4 quarts with a tablespoon of salt. When water is boiling, cook pasta until "al dente". While pasta is cooking, slice sausages into bite-size pieces and add to simmering sauce.

6. Drain pasta and return to pot, reserving a quarter cup of pasta water. Pour sauce into pot with pasta. Add pasta water. Toss well. Taste and add salt and pepper as needed.

7. Platter and top with Parmigiano-Reggiano. Garnish with Italian parsley.

8. Take off your apron quick and join the table before it is devoured.

Suggested Wine: *Sangiovese*

Sangiovese is one of the three noble grapes of Italy and is produced widely through central Italy, especially in Tuscany. The wine we've chosen here comes from an area of Tuscany known as Montecucco, which is located just west of Montalcino (where the great Brunello's are made). Some of my favorite Tuscan wines come from this area. They most often have a juicy, fruit forward character to them.

Frankie's recommendation: *Scarafone 'Montecucco' Rosso*

Frankie's Tips:

♦ If you want the sauce to be even richer, you can increase the cream and decrease the tomato sauce in equal amounts.

♦ Another option is to add a splash of wine. I would add it to the pan before the cream and use it to deglaze the pan. White wine would be my preference as it brightens flavors more than red.

♦ If you'd prefer to have the sausage more fully incorporated, remove it from its casing before cooking, and cook it as you would ground meat. Either way is excellent!

Farmer's Market Pasta

This is what the Italian's call a Giardiniera, or Garden Vegetable sauce. I've chosen to name my version "Farmer's Market Pasta" because I love to support the local farmers and I believe that local farmer's markets are are one of the best places to buy fresh and ful-flavored local produce.

Recipes for Giardiniera sauces are very flexible. You can use whatever fresh, seasonal vegetables that you like. Often the base sauce would be a standard tomato or Marinara sauce. I've chosen to do this version with our un-cooked Pomodoro sauce which is a little lighter and fresher.

5-6 servings

1 pound bow-tie or pasta of your choice

1 recipe Pomodoro Sauce (page 105)

fresh vegetables of your choice--cut into bite size peieces

Extra Virgin olive oil (to toss vegetables with)

Parmesan or other hard Italian cheese--grated or curled

fresh herb of your choice for garnish

1. Prepare Pomodoro sauce and set aside. Its even better if made a day ahead and refrgerated overnight.

2. Toss vegetables with olive oil and cook until tender (see Frankie's Tips).

3. Heat 4 quarts of water and add a tablespoon of salt when it begins to boil. Cook pasta until al dente. Reserve 1/4 cup of pasta water before draining.

4. While pasta is cooking, combine sauce and veggies and warm gently over low heat. Salt and pepper to taste.

5. When pasta is al dente, add to sauce along with the 1/4 cup of reserved pasta water. Toss together.

6. Garnish with cheese and herbs.

7. Tell God "mille grazie" for the delicious meal that is going to make you vibrant and healthy!

Suggested Wine: *Nebbiolo*

The name Nebbiolo comes from the root word nebbia which means fog in Italian. It hales from the northern Italian region of Piedmont where the fog sits upon the valleys and hillsides throughout the autumn, slowing the ripening process, and developing great depth of character.

Frankie's recommendation:
Proprieta Sperino "Uvaggio" Rosso Nebbiolo

Frankie's Tips:

♦ If the weather is nice, consider grilling your vegetables on the barbecue! This is my favorite way to cook them for optimal flavor. If you don't have a vegetable grilling pan for your barbecue, then cut the vegetables in larger slices for grilling and then cut them smaller afterwards. You could also skewer them.

♦ Another good method is to cook them in a grill pan with raised ridges. If you don't have one, any sauté pan will work.

♦ Depending on the season, some of my favorite veggies for this are asparagus, peppers, zucchini or other squash, eggplant, broccoli raab, and onions (small onions like Cipollini's are perfect).

Pasta with Wild Mushroom Sauce

This sauce invokes dreams of mushroom hunting in the woods of Piedmont or Tuscany; finding fresh Porcini mushrooms, hidden treasures on the cool, damp forest floor. This sauce has a rich, savory, comforting flavor—perfect for a chilly evening with a glass of red wine—and a meaty character even though it contains no meat (however it is also wonderful with Italian sausage added).

Not likely you'll find fresh Porcini mushrooms, but dried ones will work well. For the other mushrooms I've noted various options. If there is not much available, look to see if there is a package of dried-assorted wild mushrooms. I recently saw that Costco had a very large jar for an excellent price.

We tested many, many variations of this recipe—white wine, red wine, Marsala wine, beef stock, chicken stock, anchovies, cream, sour cream, goat cheese, and various herbs. I really think you'll adore what we've come up with. Raise a toast to my health as you enjoy this fabulous dish!

5-6 servings

2 tablespoons butter

2 tablespoons olive oil or Truffle oil

2 shallots—diced (or 1/2 cup red onion)

1 ounce dried Porcini mushrooms—soaked in 1 cup hot water / 30 minutes

3/4 pound white button or Crimini mushrooms—sliced thick or quartered

1/2 lb. (or 1-1/2 ounce dried) wild mushrooms—such as Shiitake and Oyster—rough chopped

3-4 garlic cloves—chopped fine

2 tablespoons fresh parsley—chopped (plus additional for garnish)

1 tablespoon fresh rosemary—minced

1 teaspoon salt / fresh ground pepper

3/4 cup Marsala wine

3/4 cup heavy cream

1-1/2 cup chicken stock

1 tablespoon balsamic vinegar

1 cup canned Tomato Sauce (or Marinara)

pinch crushed red peppers (optional)

1 pound pasta—such as campanelle, (my favorite), penne or pappardelle

parmesan (preferably Parmigiano-Reggiano)-- grated or curled

1. Heat the butter and oil over medium-high heat in a heavy-bottomed Dutch oven or a large deep skillet.

2. Sauté the shallot until it begins to soften.

3. Add all mushrooms and toss with oil and butter. Allow to cook one minute. Toss well with a wooden spoon and cook an additional minute.

4. Add the garlic, fresh parsley, rosemary, salt and several twists of black pepper. Toss well and cook two to three minutes until garlic is fragrant and mushrooms are getting brown.

5. Add the Marsala wine and cook one minute.

6. Add cream, chicken stock, balsamic vinegar and tomato sauce. Bring to a boil. Reduce to a simmer and cook for 12 to 15 minutes until sauce thickens slightly. Taste sauce and adjust seasonings to taste.

7. While the sauce is simmering, bring a large pot of water to boil over high heat. When the water is boiling add one tablespoon of salt.

8. Cook pasta until nearly al dente. Reserve about a 1/4 cup of pasta water before draining.

9. Drain pasta and return to the pasta pot. Stir the sauce into the pasta and pour in the reserved pasta water. Cook over medium heat for about 2 minutes, stirring constantly.

10. Serve up with parmesan and garnish with chopped Italian parsley.

Suggested Wine: *Chianti Classico Riserva*

Chianti which is designated as *Classico* come from the heart of Chianti, that land which is considered to be the best that the region has to offer. *Riserva* wines are made from the best-of-the-best grapes and are aged longer than other Chianti Classico. This particular Chianti, *Il Grigio*, displayed a certain earthy character which we felt perfectly complemented the earthiness of the mushrooms.

Frankie's recommendation: *San Felice 'Il Grigio' Chianti Classico Riserva*

Frankie's Tips:

♦ At the restaurant we use dried Porcini mushrooms and a blend of white mushrooms, Crimini, Portobello, Shiitake and Oyster mushrooms. According to my research, white mushrooms (also known as button mushrooms), Crimini mushrooms and Portobellos are all essentially of the same family of common mushrooms, only at various stages of maturity and flavor development.

♦ When prepping Shiitakes, you'll need to remove the stems which is very tough and woody.

♦ For maximum flavor, Porcini mushrooms are a key to the recipe. Shiitake mushrooms are also very rich and woodsy. I would highly recommend using them. Oyster mushrooms have a fairly delicate flavor. Other possibilities if you can find them, and are willing to put out some dough (and we're not talkin' pizza dough), would be Chanterelles and Morels. I have never tried the sauce with either but can only imagine how good it would be. If you were willing to mortgage your house to put this over the top, shaved black truffles would send it into orbit. But one thing you can do to get a little of that flavor is to use Truffle oil instead of regular olive oil.

♦ An additional step you can do to maximize mushroom flavor is to add back part of the water (which I would now call a broth) in which you soaked the Porcini mushrooms. If you do however, you will need to cook the sauce longer to evaporate the additional liquid.

Pasta with Pumpkin-Sausage Sauce

Pumpkin with pasta and sausage? So you think I've gone a little "pazzo" in the head, heh!? Too much grappa you are thinking. Well I am here to tell you that this is one of the most delizioso pasta dishes you have ever had! And so perfect for autumn. And to make it even more enticing, it is easy to prepare. I like this with spicy Chicken Italian Sausage. Of course you may use the pork stuff. So what are you waiting for? It's time to get in the kitchen!

Serves 6

4 tablespoons olive oil

1 pound of spicy Italian Sausage (chicken or pork) - casings removed

3/4 cup chopped onion

2 tablespoons chopped fresh sage

2-3 cloves of garlic—minced

1-1/4 cup dry white wine (such as Pinot Grigio)

pinch of saffron (optional)

1—15 oz. can pumpkin puree

1– 1/2 cup low-sodium chicken stock

1/2 teaspoon salt

fresh ground black pepper

freshly grated Parmesan Cheese (preferably Parmigiano-Reggiano)

1 pound hearty pasta—such as rigatoni, or papparadelle

1. Heat 1 tablespoon of the olive oil in a deep sauté pan over medium-high heat. Add the sausage and cook until it begins to brown. As it cooks, chop it relatively fine with a metal spatula or wooden spoon.

2. Reduce heat to medium. Add remaining oil and heat briefly. Add onion and sage. Sauté 5 minutes, stirring often, until most of the pink is gone from sausage.

3. Add garlic, and cook until onions begin to brown and garlic is fragrant—2-3 minutes.

4. Add white wine and cook for 8 minutes, using your spatula to scrape any browned-bits from the bottom of the pan (lot's of flavor there!).

5. Add pumpkin and cook for 2 minutes. Add chicken stock and bring to a boil over medium-high heat. Add optional saffron if desired.

6. Reduce heat to a simmer and cook for 30 minutes. Add salt and several turns of pepper. Taste and adjust seasoning as needed.

7. While sauce is cooking, bring a large pot to a boil over high heat and add a tablespoon of salt. When Pumpkin sauce has about 8-10 minutes remaining, cook your pasta until nearly al dente. Reserve about a 1/4 cup of pasta water before draining.

8. Drain pasta and return to the pasta pot. Stir the sauce into the pasta and add reserved pasta water. Cook over medium heat for 2 minutes, stirring constantly.

9. Serve up with freshly grated parmesan and garnish with a sprig of fresh sage.

Suggested Wine: *Valpolicella Ripasso*

There is a wine made in Veneto called Amarone which is made from grapes which are dried on mats for 6-8 weeks, yielding a very big, rich wine. *Ripasso* means repass in Italian. It is made by repassing light, young drinking Valpolicella with the leftover lees from the Amarone production. This gives the *Ripasso* a deeper, richer character than your every day drinking Valpolicella.

Frankie's recommendation: *Villalta Valpolicella Ripasso*

Frankie's Tips:

♦ The sage component in this sauce is fairly subtle. Though I like sage a lot, I did not want to compete with the other flavors. If you really love sage, feel free to add another tablespoon during step two. Adding at this time will give you a better flavor than if you decide later that you want more and add it raw. If adding later, I recommend that you sauté it in a little oil first.

♦ If you buy your sausage in links, often the packages will be less than a pound (often only 12 ounces). This is no big deal if you want to use just one package.

♦ I liked the addition of a pinch saffron to my sauce. Saffron can be added to a cup of the water and heated to dissolve it, or you can crush the threads with a mortar and pestle, or use a simple method of placing it on a cutting board and crushing it with the side of a chef's knife.

Spaghetti with Sardines and fried Capers

Many people think they do not like sardines. But if you try this pasta you might have second thoughts. Every now and then you come across a dish that is unlike anything you've ever had, and it blows you away with how good it is. That's how this Sicilian inspired pasta was for me. I recommend you try on a nice spring or summer day. This is an easy recipe to cut in half if there are just two or three of you.

Serves 5-6

1 pound spaghetti

1/3 cup pure olive oil

1/4 cup capers—
rinsed and patted dry

1/3 cup fresh dill—chopped

1-1/2 cups bread crumbs—made
from stale Italian bread or baguette
(*see Frankie's Tips)

4-5 cloves fresh garlic—pressed

2 cans (3.75 oz.) sardines in oil

1/2 teaspoon salt
(preferably sea salt)

fresh ground black pepper

1. To prepare the bread crumbs, place 5-6 slices day old Italian Bread in food processor with blade. Process until coarsely chopped (see Frankie's Tips).

2. Pre-prep and measure all remaining ingredients (the French call this "mise en place" which means "to have in place").

3. Cook spaghetti in 3-4 quarts water with one tablespoon of salt.

4. Meanwhile, heat oil over medium heat until it begins to shimmer. Fry capers in oil until to they begin to burst open (this is called "blooming); about 2 minutes. Transfer with a slotted spoon paper towels to drain.

5. Place bread crumbs in the same skillet and toast, stirring frequently until golden, about 2-3 minutes. Transfer to a bowl and toss with the capers and half of the dill.

6. With skillet still on medium heat, add sardines with their oil. After one minute, add pressed garlic. Cook one additional minute.

7. When pasta is nearly "al dente", reserve 3/4 cup of pasta water before draining. Drain pasta.

8. Add a third of the reserved pasta water to the skillet and loosen up any bits stuck to the bottom of the pan.

9. Add pasta to skillet along with remaining pasta water, salt and several twists of black pepper.

10. Toss until pasta is coated and sauce is slightly thickened, 1-2 minutes.

11. Serve topped with bread crumb mixture and the remaining dill.

Suggested Wine: *Italian Chardonnay*

Most New World Chardonnay's would be too rich and creamy for this dish. But generally speaking, Italian Chardonnays are crisper and leaner. Such is the case with this wine, which is produced in the hills of Umbria by the Antinori Family. The flavors work very well with the complexities of this pasta dish.

Frankie's recommendation: *Castello della Sala "Bramito" Chardonnay*

Frankie's Tips:

♦ I rarely have old, stale bread—but fresh bread will not process well into breadcrumbs. To solve this problem, place bread in a 200º F oven for 3-5 minutes to dry it out.

♦ When preparing crumbs in the food processor, use short, 2-3 second bursts until the bread crumbs are coarsely chopped (you want them a bit coarser than store bought bread crumbs).

♦ I don't recommend substituting extra virgin olive oil because it will not stand up to the heat. The oil from the sardines will provide plenty of flavor!

♦ In this recipe, as with most others, I talk about cooking the pasta until nearly "al dente". This is especially important when dealing with thinner pastas like spaghetti or angel hair (capellini), because these pastas will overcook very quickly—and because they will continue to cook some in the skillet with the other ingredients.

Linguine with Tuscan Clam Sauce

This recipe is similar to a white clam sauce except that it has the addition of crushed tomatoes. I find the result to be more delicious; more satisfying than either a white or red clam sauce. It can be made entirely from fresh clams, or with canned clams for a simple weeknight meal.

Serves 5-6

60 fresh littleneck clams
(the smaller the better)

3/4 cup white wine

1/4 teaspoon crushed red pepper

3 tablespoons olive oil

2/3 cup yellow onion

3-4 cloves of garlic--minced or pressed

1-1/4 cup crushed tomatoes--drained (or
a 14.5 ounce can of diced tomatoes)

3 tablespoons fresh Italian parsley--
chopped (plus extra for garnish)

1-1/2 tablespoon fresh oregano
(or 2 teaspoons dried)

1/2 teaspoon salt (preferably sea salt)

fresh ground black pepper

1 pound linguine pasta

1. Scrub the clams and discard any with broken shells. Place in a colander to drain.

2. Add wine to a deep sided skillet along with a half cup water. Add clams and crushed red peppers.

3. Cover skillet and bring to a boil over high heat, shaking the pan occasionally. Boil until clams just begin to open, about 3 to 4 minutes. Using a slotted spoon, transfer clams to a bowl and set aside.

4. Strain the remaining broth into another bowl by pouring it through a sieve lined with a paper towel.

5. Reserve 18 or more clams whole. With remaining clams, remove meat from shells and chop. Set aside.

6. Cook linguine until al dente. Drain and set aside.

7. While pasta is cooking, add the olive oil to the pan and place over medium heat. Sauté onions until softened. Add garlic and sauté briefly. Reduce heat and add tomatoes, parsley, oregano, salt and pepper.

8. Add back the remaining broth along with the chopped and whole clams. Cook for one minute.

9. Add pasta and toss. Arrange on platter with whole clams on top. Top with additional parsley.

Frankie's Tips:

♦ Clams that are purchased at a market have been purged of sand. If you dug the clams yourself, soak them in a bucket of salted water (1 cup of salt per 3 quarts of water). Add 1/4 cup cornmeal to water (the cornmeal will purge them of sand). Soak in the refrigerator for a couple of hours or overnight, changing the water at least once. Do not use fresh water, it will kill the clams.

♦ For a quick and simple weeknight dinner with canned clams, substitute 3 - 6.5 ounce cans of chopped clams in juice. You would then sauté the onions and garlic first; and then add the white wine and clam juices (no water) and simmer for a few minutes over low heat to reduce slightly. Then add remaining ingredients, including chopped clams.

♦ Most Italians do not believe in adding cheese to seafood pastas (to some it is sacrilege). I like it without. But if you really like your cheese, consider adding some finely grated parmesan to the sauce before removing from heat. It will thicken it slightly and add a nice zip.

Suggested Wine: *Vermentino*

The Vermentino grape is grown throughout the western Mediterranean where it goes by different names. In Italy, it is primarily grown in three areas: the island of Sardinia, the seaside region of Liguria, and in Bolgheri, a coastal area of Tuscany, where my recommended wine comes from. The vines are often grown on slopes facing the sea where they can benefit from the additional reflected light. The wine works particularly well with seafood, especially shell fish.

Guado al Tasso is a highly esteemed estate owned by the reknowned Antinori family.

Frankie's recommendation: *Guado al Tasso Vermentino*

Mediterranean Shrimp Linguine

On the previous page I wrote about how most Italians consider it sacrilege to eat cheese with seafood. And yet here I am pairing shrimp with Feta cheese. The inspiration for this dish came from a dish I had at a local restaurant of prawns, baked with tomatoes and capers topped with Feta cheese. It was so delicious that I created a pasta out of it. It can be found on our spring menu at Frankie's. It's one of my favorites, and one of our best selling seasonal menu items.

Serves 5-6

1 pound linguine pasta

1/2 cup extra virgin olive oil

10 to 12 ounces of shrimp--peeled and deveined--tails off

2 lemons--one juiced and one cut in wedges

1/3 cup capers--rinsed of brine and patted dry

1/2 cup Calamata olives--pitted and coarsely chopped

fresh ground black pepper

2 cups Pomodoro Sauce--see recipe on page 83

4 ounces Feta cheese--crumbled

Itatlian parsley--chopped for garnish

an extra large measure of love

1. Prepare Pomodoro sauce. This can be done a day or two ahead if you like--which actually makes the flavor even better.

2. Begin water for pasta—3-4 quarts with a tablespoon of salt added after the water begins to boil.

3. Heat 2 tablespoons of the olive oil in a large sauté pan or straight sided skillet over medium heat. Add shrimp and sauté until nearly opaque.

4. Add about a quarter cup of the lemon juice, along with the capers and Calamata olives and a few quick twists of black pepper. Cook until shrimp are a nice white-coral color, but still moist. Add Pomodoro sauce and turn off heat.

5. Cook linguine until nearly al dente. Drain, reserving about a quarter cup of the pasta water.

6. Add to linguine to shrimp and sauce mixture. Add remaining olive oil and and pasta water. Warm over medium heat until sauce is hot through.

7. Platter and garnish with lemon wedges and parsley.

Frankie's Tips:

♦ Unless you know how to devein shrimp, I suggest you purchase shrimp which have been peeled and deveined. If they come "tails-on", I suggest removing them. The only other tip here is to not overcook your shrimp which causes them to shrink excessively and become dry and rubbery.

Suggested Wine: *Morellino di Scansano*

This delightful red is grown in a viticultural region near the south coast of Tuscany. It is made from Sangiovese grapes, but tends to have brighter fruit than wines grown in the hotter interior. I've tried to sell it at the restaurant but nobody knows what it is, and it is such a tongue twister that nobody buys it. Such a pity.

Frankie's recommendation: *La Mozza 'I Perazzi' Morellino di Scansano*

Rhonda in Positano on the Amalfi Coast

Fisherman's Pasta

When we were in the Cinque Terre, along the coast of Liguria, we had these delightful seafood pastas which I desired to re-create. I searched and searched for recipes to no avail, and then I figured out that it was just way too simple to be true. All I had to do was take the leftover Fisherman's Soup (aka Cacciuccio--see recipe page 50), and use it for my pasta sauce. I added some mussels and clams, common to those dishes. As I devoured it, I was transported in my mind back to that magical place.

Serves 5-6

1 pound linguine pasta

1/2 cup white wine

2 tablespoons extra virgin olive oil

juice of 1/2 lemon

1 pound fresh shellfish in shells (clams, mussels or some of each)

3 cups leftover Fisherman's soup

1 tablespoon fresh Italian parsley-- chopped

an extra large portion of generosity

1. Scrub the clams and/or mussels and discard any with broken shells. Place in a colander to drain (also see Frankie's Tips on page 130 regarding cleaning clams).

2. Add wine, olive oil and lemon to a deep sided skillet along with a 1/4 cup water. Add clams and mussels.

3. Cover skillet and bring to a slow boil over high heat, shaking the pan occasionally. Boil until clams and/or mussels just begin to open, about 3 to 4 minutes. Using a slotted spoon, transfer shell fish to a bowl and set aside.

4. While shell fish are cooking, bring 3-4 quarts water to a boil. Add tablespoon of salt. Cook linguine until less than al dente.

5. While pasta is cooking, simmer and reduce any remaining broth (from the shell fish), by half. Add soup. Then add shell fish back into skillet and heat.

6. Add cooked linguine and parsley to skillet Stir and cook together for a couple of minutes. Serve with pride.

Frankie's Tips:

♦ The soup recipe allows for variations of seafood. If you used clams or mussels in the soup, you could omit them here of course. Feel free to add or delete types of seafood to your taste.

♦ When you add the "nearly" al dente pasta to the sauce and cook it for a couple more minutes, you allow it to add some of its starch to the sauce which will thicken it slightly. The pasta will also absorb the flavors of the sauce. Just be careful not to overcook the pasta. You can accomplish similar results by adding a little pasta water. Logic tells you this would make it runnier, but the starch in the pasta water acts as a thickener.

Suggested Wine: *Falanghina*

Wines from Cinque Terre are hard to find in the states, so I am recommending this delightful full-bodied, white from an area just north of Naples on the Amalfi coast of southern Italy. Falanghina has a history dating back to the Greek and Roman days. It is a delightful match with seafood.

Frankie's recommendation: *Terradora di Paolo Falanghina*

Top: Isle of Capri
Bottom: Monterossa, Cinque Terre

Baked Cheese Manicotti

This is one of those traditional comfort food dishes that you don't find as often as you used to. Yet it is easy to make and so delicious. In Italy, Manicotti are often made with crêpes as opposed to pasta, and some say it has its origins in French cooking. Among Italian Americans though, pasta has become the traditional shell. You can either buy dried manicotti shells in the grocery store or make fresh pasta.

Serves 5-6

Filling Ingredients:

1 pound ricotta cheese

1/2 cup pecorino romano cheese--grated

1/2 cup shredded mozzarella

2 eggs

3 tablespoons fresh Italian parsley--chopped (plus additional for garnish)

1 tablespoon dried oregano

2 teaspoons dried basil (or 2 tablespoons fresh)

1/4 teaspoon fresh ground pepper

1/2 teaspoon garlic powder

1/2 teaspoon salt

Other Ingredients:

12 manicotti shells or fresh pasta (see note to the right)

2 cups Marinara sauce

2 cups (about 8 ounces) mozzarella

1. If using dried pasta shells, pre-boil according to package directions.

2. Pre-heat oven to 375º F. Spread 1/2 cup of the marinara in the bottom of a 9 x 13 inch baking dish.

3. Place all filling ingredients in a mixing bowl. Mix well.

4. Spoon filling into shells (see Frankie's Tips); or if using fresh pasta sheets, place filling near front edge of the sheet and roll away from you, as if rolling a cigar (see note below). Place seam side down in the baking dish.

5. Spread remaining marinara sauce over manicotti. Top with mozzarella cheese. Cover with foil and bake 30 minutes. Remove foil and bake an additional 10 minutes.

6. Garnish with grated parmesan or pecorino romano if desired, and chopped parsley.

Pasta for Manicotti and Cannelloni:

You may use store bought tubular pasta shells (usually labeled Manicotti), or use fresh pasta. You can find large fresh pasta sheets at stores such as Cash & Carry (we buy fresh 8x10 inch pasta sheets from our supplier which we cut in quarters). Or you can make your own fresh pasta and cut them into 5 inch lengths. If using fresh pasta they do not need to be boiled prior to use.

If using fresh pasta sheets, arrange them so that the short side faces you. And then roll them away from you.

Frankie's Tips:

♦ This is best with homemade Marinara but for a quick dinner, purchase your favorite brand.

♦ Instead of spooning filling into shells, you can also place the filling in a gallon zip lock bag, cut off the corner and use it like a piping bag to squeeze filling into shells (or use a piping bag).

♦ You could do a number of simple but tasty variations on this such as substituting some Goat Cheese for some of the ricotta, or adding some chopped prosciutto to the cheese mixture.

Suggested Wine: *Aglianico*

This well priced wine is a gem. Aglianico, which is grown primarily in the southern Italian region of Campania, is considered one of the three noble grape varieties of Italy. It can make a huge wine, but for pizza or pasta I prefer the versions with less oak ageing, such as this one. The wine is still dry but with lovely fruit.

Frankie's recommendation: *Feudi di San Gregorio "Rubrato"*

Roasted Vegetable Manicotti

This is a dish which we serve on our summer menu and I always look forward to it. The vegetables listed in the recipe are what we use at the restaurant. But you can use any vegetables that you are partial to. Instead of marinara sauce we use a creamy-pomodoro sauce which is just fabulous!

Serves 6

Filling Ingredients:

1 medium to large zucchini or summer squash

1 red bell peppers

1 yellow bell peppers

1-1/2 cups mushrooms--sliced

1/2 large red onions--diced (leave uncooked)

3 - 4 cloves fresh garlic--pressed

2 tablespoons fresh Italian Parsley--chopped (plus additional for garnish)

12 ounces ricotta cheese

1/2 cup pecorino romano cheese--grated

1/2 cup parmesan cheese--grated

2 eggs

1 teaspoon salt

1/4 teaspoon fresh ground pepper

Other Ingredients:

14 manicotti shells or fresh pasta*
*see note about Pasta for Manicotti and Cannelloni on page 116

2 cups Pomodoro Sauce*
*see recipe page 105

1 cup Alfredo Sauce*
*see Frankie's Tips page 119

1. See notes under "Pasta for Manicotti and Cannelloni", and "Frankie's Tips" on page 126.

2. "Pre-heat oven to 450º F. If using dried pasta shells, pre-boil according to package directions.

3. Slice zucchini. Cut round pieces in quarters (small pieces in half). Place in a bowl.

4. Core and seed bell peppers. Cut in pieces roughly 1/2 inch square pieces. Add to bowl with zucchini.

5. Roughly chop mushrooms (approximately 1/2 x 1/2 inch pieces). Add to other veggies.

6. Toss vegetables with a light amount of olive oil and place on a baking sheet. Roast in oven, stirring periodically until peppers are slightly tender--about 15 to 20 minutes. Reduce oven Temperature to 375º F.

7. Cool vegetables. Then place in a mixing bowl and toss with red onions, garlic and parsley.

8. In a separate mixing bowl stir together cheeses, eggs, salt and pepper. Fold vegetables into cheese mixture.

9. Blend together the Pomodoro and Alfredo sauces and place 1/2 cup of it in the bottom of a baking dish.

10. Spoon mixture into shells; or if using fresh pasta sheets, place filling near the front edge of the sheet and roll gently away from you. Press edges of pasta together and place manicotti in a baking dish.

11. Pour remaining sauce over the top. Cover with foil and bake 45 minutes at 375º F.

12. Garnish with grated parmesan or romano if desired, and chopped parsley, or favorite herb of your choice.

Frankie's Tips:

♦ When we make these at the restaurant, we like to make them larger and fatter than our normal manicotti. This can only be accomplished if using fresh pasta. If you do, cut the sheets so they are 6-7 inces long and spread the filling over most of the sheet (leaving an inch uncovered on the far end of the sheet). Then roll them away from you.

Suggested Wine: *Primitivo*

Primitivo comes from the Italian region of Apulia--the heel of the Italian boot. DNA tests have shown that the grape is the biological parent of the Zinfandel grape in America. Primitivo tends to be a little spicier, and not as jammy as Zinfandel.

Frankie's recommendation: *Cantele Primitivo*

Chicken Cannelloni Florentine

This is one of the most popular dishes we serve at Frankie's and one of my personal favorites. Cannelloni originated in Palermo, Sicily. They are made by rolling a filling inside a pasta sheet, or filling a tubular pasta shell. The filling usually contains ricotta with meat or poultry, and often spinach. Typically cannelloni are then baked in a tomato or cream sauce or even a béchamel. Our version is topped with both marinara and a touch of cream sauce. I've shown a recipe for a small batch of Alfredo sauce in the Frankie's Tip's notes below.

Serves 5-6

Filling Ingredients:

3 cups chicken--cooked and diced
(see step 3 and Frankie's Tips)

3 cups chopped fresh spinach

1-1/2 cups Ricotta cheese

3/4 cup fresh Parmesan--grated

1-1/2 tablespoon chopped Italian Parsley (plus additional for garnish)

3-4 cloves fresh garlic--pressed

1/2 teaspoon garlic powder

3/4 teaspoon salt

Other Ingredients:

12 manicotti shells or fresh pasta*
*see note about Pasta for Manicotti and Cannelloni on page 116

2 cups Marinara Sauce

3/4 cup Alfredo Sauce*
*see Frankie's Tips

1. If using dried pasta shells, pre-boil according to package directions.

2. Pre-heat oven to 375º F. Spread 1/2 cup of the marinara in the bottom of a baking dish.

3. Dice chicken into approximately 1/8 to 1/4 inch pieces and place in a large mixing bowl.

4. Add all remaining filling ingredients and stir together.

5. Spoon filling into shells; or if using fresh pasta sheets, place filling near the front edge of the sheet and roll away from you, as if rolling a cigar (see note about Pasta for Manicotti and Cannelloni on page 116). Place Cannelloni seam side down in the baking dish.

6. Spread remaining Marinara sauce over the top of the Cannelloni. Cover with foil and bake for 40 minutes.

7. Heat Alfredo sauce in a pan over gentle heat. Drizzle over the top of the baked Cannelloni. Garnish with additional Parmesan if desired, and chopped parsley.

Frankie's Tips:

♦ You can use either white or dark chicken, depending on your preference (or a mix of both as we do at Frankie's). Canned chicken is okay but I prefer to to dice up boneless chicken breasts or thighs. If you cook them just prior to use, allow them to cool before adding other ingredients.

♦ I actually like the chicken pretty finely diced. The filling holds together better and I prefer the texture. At the restaurant we actually dice it a little larger than I prefer, or the customers start to ask "where's the chicken?"

♦ To make a small batch of Alfredo Sauce, simmer a pint of heavy cream over low heat with a little garlic and/or garlic powder. Reduce by about 1/4 (the sauce should easily coat back of a spoon). Toss in a small handful of grated Parmesan. Salt to taste.

Suggested Wine: *Barbera d'Alba*

I adore this Barbera producer run by three sisters in Piemonte. Their old-fashioned father had no intentions of passing his winery down to a daughter unless she married a winemaker; but the strong willed girls made a bet with papa and proved they were more than capable. All three sisters remain involved in the winery today.

Frankie's recommendation: *Tre Donne Barbera d'Alba*

Lasagne al Forno

If you were to have Lasagne in central or northern Italy it would likely be *Lasagne Bolognese*, made with Bolognese and Bechamel sauces, and often with spinach pasta. But if you were in the south, where much of our Italian-American food heritage originates from, then it would more likely be made with a meat ragu and tomato sauce, such as this recipe. I love both styles. This is the version we sell in the restaurant. I will put the recipe for Lasagne Bolognese in a future cook book.

Serves 8-10

Cheese Mixture:

2 pounds ricotta cheese

4 eggs--beaten

4 ounces (about 1 cup) mozzarella cheese

1/2 cup parmesan cheese--grated (preferably Parmigiano Reggiano)

1/2 cup pecorino romano--grated

1/4 cup fresh Italian parsley—chopped

1 teaspoon fresh ground black pepper

1 teaspoon garlic salt

Other ingredients:

1 box (16) lasagne sheets (see Frankie's Tip's)

2-1/2 cups Marinara sauce (recipe page 98)--see Frankie's Tip's

6 cups Sicilian Meat Sauce (recipe page 100)

12 ounces (about 3 cups) mozzarella cheese

Cheese Mixture preparation and pre-prep:

1. If making the sauces just prior to the lasagne, allow to cool. Measure out amount needed need and save remaining sauce for future use.
2. Thoroughly mix cheese mixture ingredients in a bowl.

Assembly:

1. This recipe has five layers of pasta with four layers of cheese and meat sauce layered in between. There is additional sauce (see Frankie's Tip's) under the first pasta layer and on top of the top layer. It is finished with a layer of mozzarella cheese on top when it is almost done baking.
2. Pre-heat oven to 375º F. Place one cup of Marinara Sauce in the bottom of baking dish or lasagne pan.
3. Place 3 lasagne sheets atop the sauce. With a rubber spatula, spread 1/4 of the cheese mixture (about 2.5 cups), on top of the pasta. Then top with 1/4 of the Sicilian Meat Sauce (about 1-1/2 cups).
4. Repeat step 3, three additional times.
5. Top with final layer of pasta (this layer will probably be 4 sheets). Top with the last 1-1/2 cups of Marinara Sauce.
6. Cover with foil. Bake for one hour. Check internal temperature to ensure it is at 150º F or higher.
7. Remove foil. Top with remaining Mozzarella cheese and return to oven for about 12 - 15 minutes until mozzarella is melted and browned to your liking.
8. Cool for 15 minutes before cutting and serving.

Suggested Wine: *Chianti*

I am happy to know the gentleman who makes this Chianti. In addition to being a fine winemaker, he is the in-country liaison in Italy for one of my favorite importers, Small Vineyards. SV only imports from very small producers, people who love their land and hand harvest their grapes. On our last visit to Italy, Antonio gave us a tour of some of their wineries and had dinner with us. He is a class act!

Frankie's recommendation: *Antonio Sanguinetti Chianti DOC*

Frankie's Tips:

♦ At the restaurant we use both our Siclian Meat sauce and Marinara. This is easy for us because we have both readily available. To simplify this, you could use just meat sauce. The only issue is that you will have lumps of meat below the first layer of pasta and on top of the lasagne. You can get around this by picking put the larger pieces of meat and placing them back in with the other sauce.

♦ I would highly suggest that you prepare your sauces in advance, either in the morning or a day or two in advance. It will make things much easier when it comes time to asseble the lasagne.

♦ For the pasta, you could make fresh pasta if desired (which we do at the restaurant), or use store bought noodles. If purchasing pasta, I like the "no boiling needed" noodles (I know Barilla makes these). It saves a step and the texture is perfect. Otherwise boil pasta sheets in advance of assembly.

♦ At Frankie's, we use five cheeses, including some fontina which we put on top along with the mozzarella. I omitted the fontina here to simplify things. You could simplify it further by omitting the pecorino romano, if you do not have any around, and increasing the parmesan.

♦ This is a very thick lasagne. Lasagne pans vary in size. Depending on the size you use, you may have a hard time getting it all in the pan. You can reduce ingredients a little or eliminate a layer if your pan is smaller or not deep enough. Buon appetito!

Baked Rigatoni with Sausage & Eggplant

"The lone eggplant"

It was early July and I had one lone eggplant in my garden. It would be weeks before another would even start to grow.

What to do with one eggplant? Not enough to make eggplant parmesan. So I decided to put it in a pasta. I've made pasta with eggplant before with varying levels of success. I stole the inspiration for this dish and then modified it to my liking. On the first try it turned out amazing!

6 servings

1 large eggplant (1 to 1-1/2 lbs.) cut into 3/4 inch squares

1 medium onion—finely chopped

3-4 cloves fresh garlic—pressed or minced

1/4 cup fresh basil—julienned

3/4 pound (or up to 1 pound) spicy Italian sausage

2 tablespoons extra virgin olive oil

2 tablespoons pure olive oil

28 oz. can Whole Peeled Tomatoes (preferably San Marzano style)

2 tbs. tomato paste

3/4 tsp. salt

1 pound rigatoni

1 pound fresh mozzarella—diced into 3/4 inch squares (see Frankie's Tip's)

1 cup freshly grated Parmigiano-Reggiano

1. Put on an old Godfather sound track. We're cookin' Sicilian bambino!

2. Pre-heat oven to 450 F.

3. Pre-prep and measure all ingredients. Place tomatoes in a large bowl with juices, and break up tomatoes with your hands. If sausage is in links, remove from casing.

4. Place eggplant in large bowl and toss with extra virgin olive oil. Place on a baking sheet and bake for 8 minutes. Toss with a spatula and return to oven for an additional 5 minutes. Set aside.

5. While eggplant is roasting, drizzle pure olive oil in a large, straight sided skillet. Heat over medium-high heat until oil begins to shimmer. Add sausage. Chop and stir until most of the pink is gone. Drain excess fat, and set aside with eggplant.

6. Heat water for pasta—3-4 quarts with 1 tablespoon salt.

7. Drizzle remaining pure olive oil into skillet and sauté onion until translucent. Add garlic and sauté for an additional 1 to 2 minutes.

8. Add tomatoes, basil, salt and tomato paste. Cook until sauce is pulpy and somewhat thick, approximately 12 to 15 minutes.

9. While sauce is cooking, add rigatoni to boiling water. Cook about a minute less than package directions (just shy of al dente--it will continue cooking in the oven).

10. Drain pasta and return to pasta pot. Add sauce, eggplant, sausage and 1/2 of the fresh mozzarella, and toss. Transfer to a 9x13 baking dish and top with the grated Parmigiano-Reggiano.

11. Bake 12 minutes. Top with remaining fresh mozzarella.

12. Bake additional 12 minutes, or until top is golden-brown and bubbly.

Suggested Wine: *Bolgheri Rosso*

Bolgheri is an area of Tuscany quite unique from all the others. Located near the coast, the soils are best suited for for Bordeaux-style varietals such as Cabernet, Merlot, and Syrah. This is the birthplace of the Super-Tuscan wines, most of which would overwhelm a peasant dish like this. This lighter version, which includes the above mentioned grapes plus Sangiovese, is a perfect match.

Frankie's recommendation: *LeMacchiole Bolgheri Rosso*

Frankie's Tips:

♦ Feel free to substitute spicy Chicken Italian Sausage for pork sausage. I like it just as well.

♦ This recipe calls for cooking the sausage and eggplant aside from the sauce and then mixing later. This method ensures that sausage is not overcooked (since it will receive additional cooking).

♦ Fresh mozzarella, also known as Fior Di Latte, is different than regular mozzarella. It is fresher, softer, and far more perishable than regular mozzarella. It also has a higher moisture content. For more information, see the notes about cheeses under *Pizza Ingredients (page 74)*.

Frankie's Baked Macaroni and Cheese
With Applewood Smoked Bacon

This is not an Italian pasta dish. It is as American as apple pie. But who cares! It is so darn good that it had to have a place in my cook book. At Frankie's, we serve this on our autumn menu when people are REALLY in the mood for comfort food! It sells better than any other seasonal menu item we serve.

6 to 8 servings

1/4 pound smoked bacon (preferably applewood smoked)

1-1/4 pounds macaroni pasta

10 tablespoons butter

1/2 pound fontina cheese--shredded

1-1/2 pounds cheddar cheese--diced in 1/2 inch cubes

1/2 cup onion--very finely minced

1/2 cup, plus 2 tablespoons flour

3 cups milk (2% or whole)

1/2 tablespoon salt

1/2 teaspoon pepper (preferably white pepper)

2 large eggs

chili powder

3/4 cups bread crumbs (homemade are best--see Frankie's Tips)

1/4 cup freshly grated parmesan cheese

1/4 cup pure olive oil

1. Pre-heat oven to 350° F. Lightly butter a 9 x 12 baking dish.
2. Fry the bacon. Cool, chop and set aside.
3. Bring 4 to 5 quarts water to boil in a large pot. When boiling, add a tablespoon of salt. Cook pasta until a little less than al dente.
4. Drain pasta and place in a large bowl. Add bacon, fontina and half of the cubed cheddar to bowl. Toss well.
5. Melt remaining butter in a large sauté pan over medium heat. Sauté onions until soft. Reduce heat and whisk in flour until smooth. Cook, and continue whisking, until flour mixture turns a light brown color.
6. Slowly whisk in milk to prevent lumps. Add salt and pepper. Cook over medium heat until slightly thickened.
7. Add the remaining half of cheddar cheese to the sauce and stir until melted. Reserve 1/2 cup of the cheese sauce.
8. Add cheese sauce to the macaroni (except for the 1/2 cup reserved) and toss together. Spread in pan.
9. Whisk eggs, then slowly add the 1/2 cup of reserved cheese sauce, whisking constantly to prevent eggs from cooking. Pour over macaroni.
10. Lightly sprinkle with chili powder. Combine bread crumbs, parmesan cheese and olive oil in a small bowl and spread over the top.
11. Bake for 25 minutes or until bubbly and golden brown. If you want the top to brown more, turn oven to broil and broil for 1 to 2 minutes (watch carefully!).
12. Be careful not to get trampled by the familiy as they rush to the dinner table.

Suggested Wine: *Montepulcino d'Abruzzo*

What really surprised me was that this dish went best with a light red wine. I had fully expected to pair it with a rich white. Montepulciano d'Abruzzo comes from the region of Abruzzo, and is naturally low in acidity. You want a younger drinking version, with little or no oak aging to pair with this dish.

Frankie's recommendation: *Villa Rocca Montepulciano d'Abruzzo*

Frankie's Tips:

♦ Old, stale bread, usually referred to as "day old bread" is best for making bread crumbs. Fresh bread does not process well into crumbs. If all you have is fresh bread, place the desired quantity of bread in a 200º F oven for a few minutes to dry it out. I prefer the texture of Italian or French-style breads, but if you don't have those, use whatever you have on hand.

♦ To prepare the bread crumbs, place 2-3 slices day old bread in food processor with blade, and using short, 2-3 second bursts, process until bread is coarsely chopped (you want them a bit coarser than store bought bread crumbs).

♦ Note that with the cheddar cheese, some is added to the pasta, and some goes into the sauce.

♦ Feel free to substitute cheeses in this recipe to make it your own. The possibilities are endless. I suggest that you primarily stay with medium-aged cheeses though. Aged (hard) cheeses do not melt as well, and young (soft) cheeses will give you a very soft texture. A few possibilities to consider are gorgonzola, cambazola, provolone, or Italian cheese with truffles in it (yum!).

♦ When serving, you can dish this out with a spoon; or if you want to serve it in large pieces as we do, you would need to allow it to cool first in order to set up, then re-warm the individual pieces.

Fresh Pasta

Making fresh, homemade pasta is a little bit of work but it is great fun and the pasta is delicious! And once you've made it a few times you get more comfortable with it, and faster and faster at the preparation.

There are several methods which can be employed... The pasta dough can be made by hand or in a food processor. I suggest starting with the food processor since the other is a little tricky to learn. As far as rolling out the pasta dough, it can be done with a dowel or roller; or it can be done using a pasta making machine. Pasta machines come in hand crank or electric versions; or if you have a Kitchenaid mixer you can buy an attachment for that. I used a hand crank machine for years and always found it a little awkward. I finally bought an attachment for my mixer and find that it make the process so much easier.

On the following pages I have listed several recipes for homemade pasta. They all begin with the same basic ingredients - flour, eggs, and sometimes salt and/or oil and possibly a little water. To this you can add flavorings if you like, suce as Roasted Red Peppers or Spinach to add both color and flavor.

Chicken Sausage Ravioli
See recipe on page 153

Fresh Egg Pasta:

2 cups all purpose flour

2 eggs

2 egg yolks

1/2 teaspoon salt

1 teaspoon olive oil

Roasted Red Pepper Pasta:

1 cup Roasted Red Bell Peppers*
*see Frankie's Tips

2 cups all purpose flour

1 egg

1 egg yolk

1/2 teaspoon salt

1 teaspoon olive oil

Lemon-Pepper Pasta:

2 tablespoons lemon juice*

2 tablespoons lemon zest*

*note: one large lemon should be adequate for zest and juice

1 teaspoon fresh ground black pepper - medium grind

2 cups all purpose flour

1 egg

2 egg yolks

1/2 teaspoon salt

1 teaspoon olive oil

Spinach Pasta:

4 ounces fresh spinach - steamed and patted dry with paper towels

2 cups all purpose flour

1 eggs

2 egg yolks

1/2 teaspoon salt

1 teaspoon olive oil

Procedure for Fresh Egg Pasta dough:

1. Place flour, eggs, yolks, salt and oil in food processor.

2. Process for 20 seconds. Stop the processor and feel the dough. It should adhere together when squeezed between your fingers (but not feel too wet and sticky). If the mixture has not begun to form a ball - gradually add a little cold water, 1 teaspoon at a time, and continue to process in short intervals until the mixture just begins to come together as a ball.

3. Remove mixture from processor and place on a lightly floured work surface. Knead with the ball of your hand, turning and folding several times, until the dough is smooth and elastic. Press into a rectangle about one inch thick. Place in a plastic bag, or wrap with plastic wrap, and set aside to rest for at least 20 minutes.

Procedure for Roasted Red Pepper Pasta:

Place roasted red pepper in food processor. Process until fairly smooth. Add remaining ingredients and proceed with steps 2-8 as listed above.

Procedure for Lemon-Pepper Pasta:

Add all ingredients and proceed with steps above.

Procedure for Spinach Pasta:

Place spinach in food processor. Process until fairly smooth. Add remaining ingredients and proceed with steps 2-8 as listed above.

Frankie's Tips:

♦ Use eggs and yolks at room temperature.

♦ The objective is to achieve a dough which has an adequate level of moisture without being too wet. If you have never made dough before, it is better to err on the side of slightly too much moisture as the dough will be easier to work with. However, this will require a little more flour on your work surface and a longer drying time before cutting.

♦ If making Roasted Red Pepper pasta, you can either use store bought peppers (which generally come in a jar), or you can roast your own (see page 76).

Procedure for rolling out pasta:

Machine method:

1. After the dough has rested, remove from plastic and cut into four pieces. Place three of the pieces back in the bag to keep from drying out. Press out the remaining piece with your hands or a rolling pin until it is under a half inch (it must be thin enough to place in the roller of pasta making machine).

2. Set pasta rolling machine at its widest setting. Feed dough into roller. Take the rolled piece and fold it into thirds like a letter. Turn 90 degrees and feed through roller again. Repeat until dough is smooth.

3. Reduce the width of the rollers by one notch. Run the dough through the machine once. Reduce the width by one additional number and run the pasta through again. Continue until you have reached desired thickness.

4. Lay the dough on a lightly floured counter or a clean, dry cloth towel. Repeat for remaining dough.

Hand rolling method:

1. Lightly flour a flat work surface at least three by three feet square.

2. After dough has rested, remove from plastic and cut into two pieces. Place one portion back in the bag to keep from drying out. If dough is damp, briefly knead it to work the moisture back in.

3. Flatten the dough with your hands to form a round disk, and place it on the floured work surface. Lightly flour the top of the dough and your rolling pin.

4. Working from the middle outward, begin to roll the dough until it is about 1/4 inch thick. Rotate the dough and continue rolling (if it sticks to work surface or your rolling pin, add more flour as needed). Continue this process until the dough is showing some transparency.

5. Lay the dough on a lightly floured counter or a clean, dry cloth towel. Repeat for remaining dough.

Procedure for cutting pasta:

Important Tip: Before you cut the pasta it must be allowed to dry until it begins to feel a bit leathery. If the pasta is too moist it will stick together. If it is too dry and brittle, it will crack. It is very likely that by the time you finish rolling all the dough, the initial sheets will be ready to use. If not, allow to dry an additional 5 to 10 minutes.

1. If sheets are longer than you desire, cut to desired length (about 10 - 14 inches is ideal).

2. Pasta may be cut by hand (a good method for wide pastas such as tagliatelle or pappardelle), or by using cutting attachments for your pasta machine.

3. If cutting by hand, loosely roll the sheet of pasta into a flat roll about 2 inches across. Place on a cutting board and using a sharp knife, cut the roll into ribbons of desired width.

4. If using a pasta machine, attach the desired cutter to the machine, and run the sheets through the cutter.

5. If you plan to use the pasta that day, lay the cut pasta flat on a lightly floured counter or a clean, dry towel. If planning to use on a future date (dried pasta will stay good for weeks), loosely wrap around your hand into nests and set out to dry completely. Store in plastic bags in refrigerator.

Frankie's Tips:

♦ I prefer the machine rolled method for rolling dough because I feel I have better control of the thickness. Some say they can get a better texture by rolling it by hand.

♦ The first time you roll out dough with a pasta machine, you will find it to be a bit of a pain. Don't give up! With a little practice, you'll be a pro in no time.

♦ If using a pasta machine for rolling dough, the initial step of rolling and folding multiple times is to help you achieve the proper smoothness - so don't skip this step. Also, when you are adjusting the settings on the roller to thin the pasta, don't skip notches. It needs to be thinned out slowly to attain the proper elasticity.

♦ Make sure you have plenty of work surface for laying out dough sheets and cut pasta. If you are tight on space, use a little creativity. Drape a clean, dry towel over a chair or cupboard door and place your pasta sheets over it to dry; or use a collapsible clothes drying rack. You can purchase special pasta drying racks but they do not hold much and can be costly.

♦ Depending on the pasta machine, the thinnest setting for the roller can be pretty thin; fine for a very delicate pasta like angel hair, but thinner than I personally like for most of my pastas. You will have to practice at coming up with a setting which gives you the delicacy or heartiness you like. Just be aware that if you leave it *too thick* it may not feed through the cutting attachment on your machine, and will need to be hand cut.

♦ Okay, one last tip. One you won't find anywhere but here! My son Noah came up with this and I've never seen anybody else do it. Are you ready for an exclusive?... Once you have passed your dough through your pasta machine a few times and have achieved the proper smoothness, run it through the roller again and stop the machine when the dough sheet is about 2/3 of the way through the roller. Then overlap the two ends of the sheet by a couple of inches, and press together, so you create one continuous sheet (like a belt sander). Place your hand within the circle created (to guide the dough). Turn the machine back on and allow the dough to circulate in a continuous cycle, occasionally changing the notch to thinner settings until you have achieved the desired setting. Is that cool or what?!

Making Fresh Ravioli

Just the idea of making fresh ravioli or tortellini is probably scary to many of you. But it is not as difficult as you might think. You'll be pretty slow at first, but so what. Just think of the reaction of your guests when they found out you made them from scratch, just for them! If you have a friend or loved one who likes to cook, this is a fun team project!

Before you tackle this though, I recommend that you've made fresh pasta a few times and feel comfortable with that. This then becomes just a natural extension of your growing culinary skills.

Ravioli Techniques and Tips:

1. You can make ravioli with any of the pasta dough recipes. Just be careful not to use too much oil or the edges will have a tendency not to adhere together.

2. When rolling out the pasta dough, you may either use the machine method or roll out by hand. If using the machine method, try to ensure that the strips of pasta dough are the full possible width of the rollers. Pasta dough should be nice and thin so roll dough out to its thinnest setting. I did notice however that the Kitchenaid dough roller attachment went even thinner than my hand roller. So on that model you may want to stop at the next to last setting.   If rolling by hand, it will take a bit of patience to get the dough thin enough. Continue rolling until the dough is nearly translucent.

3. Also, do not let the dough dry out too much or it will not adhere well when trying to seal the edges. And be careful of how much flour you put on top of the rolled pasta, especially along the edges - that too can prevent the edges from sealing properly.

4. There are various ways to cut the edges of ravioli... If you want square or triangular ravioli, you can use a knife or a pizza cutter to cut the edges. Or if you want the edges to be fluted (like the pasta shown on page 151), purchase a fluted pasta cutter at a kitchen store. These cutters are inexpensive and the finish looks great. If you want round ravioli, you can cut with a cookie cutter-- either straight or with a fluted edge. But I've found that the special ravioli cutters, available in most kitchen stores in various shapes and sizes, will work better. Another popular ravioli shape I really like is called a mezzaluna--or half moon shape--which is the shape we used for the Pear Ravioli found on page 154. These are made by folding the dough over the filling to create one straight edge, and then using a fluted pasta cutter to cut a half circle around the filling.

5. I will tell you from experience that making larger ravioli is far less time consuming than making a bunch of small ones.

6. For placing the filling on ravioli you can use a small spoon or scoop; but if you plan to make a large quantity, a pastry bag with a large tip will be quicker and easier.

7. It is important to create a good seal on the edges of the ravioli. I suggest using an egg wash (one egg beaten well with a little water), which is brushed along the edges just prior to sealing them. I also recommend that you press most of the air out around the filling. Too much trapped air can expand when cooking and cause the ravioli to burst open.

8. Ravioli can be made a day or two ahead and refrigerated, or you can even freeze them for up to several weeks. If you plan to freeze them, I suggest that you lay them out individually on a tray and place in the freezer until they are at least partially frozen. You may then gently transfer them to zip lock freezer bags.   They can be cooked from either a frozen or thawed state. Have fun!

Chicken Sausage Ravioli
With Roasted Red Pepper wrap--pictured on page 148

This is a completely original recipe. I happen to really like a good Chicken Italian Sausage. This is one of those foods where I don't feel cheated by eating the healthier version. You can serve this ravioli with a sauce but I prefer it with just a good quality extra virgin olive oil so the flavor of the ravioli shines through.

4 servings

1 recipe Roasted Red Pepper Pasta

pure olive oil

1/2 large shallot--minced

2 to 3 cloves garlic--minced

1/2 pound Chicken Italian sausage--casings removed

1 cup ricotta cheese

1/4 cup fresh grated pecorino romano cheese (plus additional to garnish pasta before serving)

1 egg yolk

1/4 cup fresh basil--julienned (plus additional for garnish)

1/4 teaspoon salt

extra virgin olive oil

Preparing Pasta and Filling:

1. Prepare pasta. Wrap in plastic wrap and set aside.
2. Drizzle pure olive oil in a large, straight sided skillet and heat over medium heat until oil begins to shimmer. Sauté shallot until translucent.
3. Add sausage to skillet. Chop and stir with a wooden spatula until most of the pink is gone. Add garlic and sauté 1 to 2 minutes more.
4. Transfer sausage mixture to a plate lined with paper towels and allow to cool to room temperature.
5. Combine ricotta and pecorino romano cheeses. Add egg yolk, basil and salt. Stir together.
6. Roll out pasta and fill as per instructions on page 152.

Finishing Ravioli:

1. Bring pasta water to a boil. Cook ravioli until they all float to the surface--about 3-4 minutes.
2. Drain and return to pot. Toss with extra virgin olive oil.
3. Plate and garnish with pecorino romano and julienned fresh basil.

Suggested Wine: *Valpolicella Classico*

Valpolicella, which means "valley of many cellars", hails from an area just north of Verona in Veneto. Its primary grape is Corvina, with the addition of Rondinella, and Molinara. The wine is light-bodied, fruity, velvety, and zesty. This dish also went well with a white wine: *Pietramala "Terre Margaritelli" Bianca del Umbria*

Frankie's recommendation: *Le Salette Valpolicella Classico*

Frankie's Tips:

♦ If this is your first time making ravioli, I suggest you read the *Ravioli Techniques and Tips* on page 152.

♦ You could make any shape of ravioli you want from these. I will tell you from experience that making larger ravioli is less time consuming.

♦ If you'd prefer a sauce with these, such as a Tomato Sauce, I suggest tossing with just enough sauce to lightly coat the pasta so you do not overwhelm the flavors of the pasta and filling.

# *Pear Ravioli*
With Sauce of Asparagus and Taleggio Cheese

We first enjoyed this dish at the home of our good friends, Ron and Cathie Barnhart, who lived in Umbria for a year. They'd experienced this dish at a little trattoria in Firenze (Florence). It was one of those memorable meals I often heard them wax on about, with a glazed look in their eyes. Ron later helped me re-test this recipe to see if we could make a great dish even better. The trattoria, Quattro Leoni, just happened to have the original recipe on their web-site. We were extremely satisfied with the results!

4 servings

Pasta and Filling Ingredients:

1 recipe fresh egg pasta

1 cup ricotta cheese

1/2 cup mascarpone cheese

1/2 cup fresh grated Parmigiano-Reggiano--loosely packed

1 cup fresh pear--pealed / diced small

1 cup pear--pureed in food processor

Sauce Ingredients:

2 ounces butter--softened

1 teaspoon flour

3 fluid ounces sweet white wine (such as Riesling)

1 cup light cream

1/2 cup taleggio cheese (or Italian sheeps milk cheese)

1/2 cup fresh grated Parmigiano-Reggiano--loosely packed

1/4 pound asparagus tips--very finely chopped

1/2 cup hazelnuts--toasted and chopped finely

Italian parsley—chopped (for garnish)

Preparing Pasta and Filling:

1. Prepare fresh egg pasta. Wrap and set aside.

2. Combine ricotta, mascarpone and parmigiano cheeses. Stir in diced and pureed pears.

3. Roll out pasta and fill as per instructions on page 152.

Preparing Sauce and Finishing Pasta:

1. If you have not prepped your hazelnuts yet, chop and place in a dry skillet over medium heat. Stir regularly and cook 2-3 minutes until fragrant. Set aside.

2. Combine the butter and flour. Melt in pan over low-medium heat.

3. Add wine. Bring to a simmer and reduce by one-third.

4. Add cream and bring to a simmer. Add taleggio cheese in small pieces. Add parmigiano and mix well until cheeses are completely melted. Add asparagus tips.

5. Taste the sauce and salt and pepper to taste.

6. Bring pasta water to a boil. Cook ravioli until they all float to the surface--about 3-4 minutes.

7. Place ravioli in sauce and toss gently to coat. Plate and garnish with chopped hazelnuts and Italian parsley.

Suggested Wine: *Gavi di Gavi*

Gavi wines are grown in Piemonte from a grape called Cortese (the Italian derivative of my name!). Piemonte also happens to be a region with large pear production. This single-vineyard Gavi di Gavi from La Meirana possesses lovely balance. It is a generous medium-bodied Gavi made in a richly textured, yet crisp style.

Frankie's recommendation: *Broglia Gavi di Gavi "La Meirana"*

Frankie's Tips:

♦ You could make any shape of ravioli you want from these. We made Mezzaluna which are half-moon shaped (see page 152 for procedure).

♦ Taleggio cheese is a semi-soft sheep's milk cheese with a very strong aroma. Some would call it a "stinky" cheese, but don't be put off by its powerful smell. It has a delicious flavor. It can be hard to find though. In the Seattle area you would need to go to a market with a large cheese selection such as Whole Foods. I actually used an Italian sheep's milk cheese which I found at Trader Joe's. It is a bit milder but we were very pleased with the results.

♦ Pears come in different varieties. We used Bosc pears which I happen to like. The pears we used were pretty small so it took about six pears. If large, it would probably only require 3-4.

♦ You can peel the pears by hand, but if you have an apple corer, that would make the job of peeling and slicing really easy. You can then take the resulting thin slices and cut them smaller.

♦ You want the flavor of the asparagus to be very subtle or it will overwhelm the dish. Buy a pound of asparagus and then you are just going to use the tip portion, which you will chop very finely.

How to make homemade Gnocchi

For years I was oblivious to the joys of gnocchi. It was really my daughter Jenna, and her love of gnocchi that sparked my interest. Now it is one of my favorites and we make it a point to have a gnocchi dish on the restaurant menu each season.

Gnocchi (pronounced nee-YOH-key) means *lumps* in Italian and they are essentially tiny dumplings. It is a traditional form of Italian pasta which dates back to the days of the Romans. Typically they are made out of potato, or sometimes out of semolina flour. Another popular variety, common in Tuscany and regions north, is Gnocchi di Spinaci e Ricotta (Spinach and Ricotta Gnocchi), which will be in a future cook book.

Gnocchi are not difficult to make but getting them just right takes a little practice. The best gnocchi are soft, light and fluffy.

Gnocchi Techniques and Tips:

There are really just two keys to making gnocchi with that desired tender, light and fluffy texture.

1. Gnocchi has flour worked into the dough. One key to successful gnocchi is to add just the right amount of flour. Too little will yield a dough that is too sticky and falls apart; and the gnocchi will be overly soft and mushy. Too much flour on the other hand will make the gnocchi dense and chewy. It is hard to tell you an exact amount because the moisture level of the potatoes and the spinach-ricotta blend can vary. So when making the gnocchi, I will instruct you to start with a certain amount of flour and then add a little more as needed.

2. The other tip is to not overwork the dough which will make it tough. This is one reason not to use your mixer or food processor to mix the dough. You want to knead the dough by hand.

Potato Gnocchi Tips:

For successful potato gnocchi there are just a few keys... one is to choose the right type of potato and the other is how you cook, and mash it.

1. The best kind of potatoes for gnocchi are Russet or other baking potatoes. Waxy types should be avoided, as should other types which are higher in moisture content (requiring too much flour).

2. Baking is the best method for cooking the potatoes. Baking causes the potatoes to lose some of their water weight which will then require less flour, yielding greater tenderness to the gnocchi. It will also give you better potato flavor.

3. When mashing you want to avoid lumpy potatoes, both because of an undesireable texture and because it can cause your dough to break apart. The best method is to use a ricer. They are inexpensive and you will also love using it when you make mashed potatoes.

Potato Gnocchi

A number of delightful recipes in which to use these gnocchi appear on the following pages. You can always purchase store bought potato gnocchi but they are not quite as good, and its fun to make your own. This is an easy recipe to double for a crowd, or if you'd like to freeze some for future use. Buon appetito!

Serves 4 as a main course or 6 as a first course

2 pounds Russet potatoes-- washed

1-1/4 cups all purpose flour--plus more as needed

1 teaspoon salt

1. Read Techniques and Tips on previous page.

2. Heat oven to 400 F. Bake the potatoes until fork tender, about 50 to 60 minutes.

3. While the potatoes are still hot, hold with a fork inserted and peel away the skin with a paring knife (the skin will re-adhere as the potato cools).

4. Rice the potatoes into a large mixing bowl and allow to cool 15 minutes.

5. Sprinkle the 1-1/4 cups flour and the salt over the potatoes. Using clean hands, work the dough until evenly mixed and the dough has a smooth consistency. If the dough feels excessively sticky, add one or two tablespoons of additional flour.

6. Flour your work surface. Also lightly flour a baking sheet (or a Silpat liner), on which to place the individual gnocchi after they are formed.

7. Divide the dough in quarters. Flour your hands, and then roll one piece of dough on the floured surface into a rope, about 5/8 inch thick.

8. Using a pastry cutter or a knife, cut each rope into 3/4 inch lengths.

9. Flour your fork or other ridge-making tool (if using a fork, hold it nearly vertical with the outer curve of the tines away from you--see photo). Press each piece of dough against the ridged surface with your index finger to make an indentation in the middle. Roll the dough down and off the ridges and let it fall to the work surface. Periodically transfer to baking sheet.

10. If you desire to freeze some or all of the gnocchi for future use, place the baking sheet in the freezer. Once gnocchi are frozen, transfer to a zip-loc freezer storage bag. Gnocchi can be cooked frozen.

11. For cooking, bring water to boil and add a tablesoon of salt. Working in batches, add gnocchi to water and cook until they rise to the surface. Remove with a slotted spoon and drain.

Potato Gnocchi
With Butter, Sage, and Parmesan Cheese

Like pasta, gnocchi can be served with a multitude of sauce variations. You will find some delightful recipes on the pages following. Yet one of the traditional and easiest ways to serve potato gnocchi is with a sauce of butter, sage, and parmesan cheese. Sometimes the simplest things are best.

Serves 4 as a main course or 6 as a first course

One recipe of Potato Gnocchi--recipe on previuos page--or 1 pound of store bought gnocchi

6 tablespoons high quality butter

12-15 fresh sage leaves--julienne cut-- plus one or more sprigs for garnish

1/2 cup (about 3/4 ounces) freshly grated Parmigiano-Reggiano--plus additional for passing at table

1. Bring 3 to 4 quarts water to boil in a large pot. When boiling, add a tablesoon of salt.

2. While water is heating, melt butter in a large sauté pan over moderate heat until the it begins to foam. Stir in sage. Remove from heat. Cover to keep warm.

3. In batches, add gnocchi to water and cook until they rise to the surface. Remove with a slotted spoon and drain.

4. When all gnocchi are cooked, add to the pan with the butter-sage mixture. Add grated parmesan. Gently toss.

5. Serve in a shallow bowl or platter. Lovingly garnish with a sprig of fresh sage. Serve at table with a hunk of Parmigiano-Reggiano and grater or a vegetable peeler for shaving.   Now that was easy!

Suggested Wine: *Umbrian Chardonnay-Sauvignon Blanc*

This wine combines the creaminess of chardonnay, which works with the butter in this dish; with the slight herbal character of Sauvignon Blanc which works well with the sage. The estate, which is one of my favorite wineries from the region of Umbria, is located between Orvieto and Todi, surrounding Lake Corbara.

Recommended Wine: *Salviano di Salviano Chardonnay-Sauvignon Blanc*

Suggested Wine: *Italian Chardonnay*

You want a touch of creaminess to match this dish. I really like this affordable Tuscan Chardonnay made by one of the best producers in the region. It fits the bill just perfectly.

Frankie's recommendation: *Isole & Olena Chardonnay "Collezione de Marchi*

Gnocchi with Chicken Sausage & Apples
With Gorgonzola Cream Sauce

This dish is an original creation by myself which we have served as an autumn seasonal dish for many years. It can be made with gnocchi but is also great with pasta such as bow-tie or rigatone. No matter how you make it, the love triangle of sausage, apples and gorgonzola cheese is like wedded bliss!

Serves 4 as a main course or 6 as a first course

1 recipe Potato Gnocchi (or one pound store bought gnocchi or pasta)

1/3 cup chopped walnuts--toasted

4 Chicken Italian sausage links (or pork if you'd prefer)

1 pint heavy cream

6 ounces gorgonzola cheese

1/2 cup white wine

1 ounce lemon juice

2 cups diced apples (I prefer Gala)

2 to 3 cloves of garlic--minced

Parmesan (preferably Parmigiano-Reggiano) - grated or curled

Chopped herb such as Italian parsley or sage for garnish

1. If making your own gnocchi, prepare as per recipe on page 157. Set aside.

2. To toast walnuts, place in a dry skillet over low to medium heat and toast, stirring occasionally until medium brown and fragrant--about 3 to 4 minutes. Set aside and wipe skillet with paper towel.

3. Add a little olive oil to the skillet and cook sausages over medium heat until exterior is well browned. Add enough water to cover the sausages about two-thirds. Bring to a brisk simmer and continue to cook, adding additional water if needed, until the sausages reach an internal temperature of 165º F. Set sausages aside to cool. Wipe out skillet.

4. Add cream to skillet and simmer over low-medium heat until reduced by about 20%. Add white wine and simmer about 2 minutes longer. Add gorgonzola cheese and lemon juice and stir in to melt cheese. Remove from heat.

5. Bring 3 to 4 quarts water to boil in a large pot for cooking gnocchi. When boiling, and add a tablesoon of salt.

6. While water is heating, slice sausages into bite size pieces. Heat a little oil in a straight-sided skillet over medium heat. Add sliced sausages and diced apples and sauté until apples begin to soften and caramelize. Add garlic.   Stir and cook one additional minute.

7. Add sauce to pan with sausage and apples. Turn to very low heat.

8. Working in batches, add gnocchi to water and cook until they rise to the surface. Remove with a slotted spoon and drain.

9. When all gnocchi are cooked, add them to the pan with the sauce, sausage and apples. Gently toss.

10. Platter and garnish with parmesan, and parsley or sage.

Gnocchi with Sausage & Sweet Peppers

I look forward to having this gnocchi every year when it arrives on our summer menu at the restaurant. Peppers just seem right for summer. We use red and yellow bell peppers. I find them to be sweeter and less pungent than green bell peppers. I also love it with rigatoni if you'd prefer with pasta.

This recipe is quite healthy for you except for maybe the sausage. Feel free to use chicken sausage which I like just as well. Did you know that red bell peppers are full of anti-oxidants and also are good for your skin? They keep you looking younger!

Serves 4 as a main course or 6 as a first course

1 recipe potato gnocchi (or one pound store bought gnocchi or rigatoni pasta)

2 tablespoons olive oil

3/4 pound spicy Italian sausage (pork sausage or chicken)

1 red bell pepper

1 yellow bell pepper

1/2 medium yellow onion

2 to 3 cloves garlic

1 quart of Marinara sauce (store bought or made from recipe on page 76)

1/2 cup Parmesan (preferably Parmigiano-Reggiano)--grated or curled

Italian parsley for garnish (optional)

1. Core the bell peppers and cut into bite-size pieces, roughly a 1/2 inch by 3/4 inch. Cut onion into bite size slivers.

2. Cook sausage in a deep sauté pan over medium heat (if sausage came in casings, remove before cooking). Transfer to paper towels to drain. Wipe out pan.

3. Bring 4 quarts water to boil in a large pot for cooking gnocchi. When boiling, add a tablespoon of salt.

4. While water is heating, heat olive oil in the sauté pan over medium-high heat. Add peppers and onions and cook until they soften. Add garlic and sauté briefly.

5. Add Marinara to pan, and return the cooked sausage to pan also. Warm over medium heat.

6. In batches, add gnocchi to water and cook until they rise to the surface. Remove with a slotted spoon and drain.

7. When all gnocchi are cooked, add to the pan with a little of the pasta water and toss with other ingredients.

8. Platter and top with parmesan cheese and garnish with parsley if desired.

Suggested Wine: _Nero d'Avola_

Nero d'Avola is a very dark skinned grape (Nero means black) and named for the Avola region in southern Sicily. It is explosive with sun-baked Mediterranean flavors, with sweet tannins and peppery plum on the palate.

The Villa Pozzi Nero d'Avola is a great value. We've released it to our wine club and have had more re-sales on this wine than any we've ever done.

Frankie's recommendation: _Villa Pozzi Nero d'Avola_

Umbrian olive trees in the morning fog

Mediterranean Chicken & Olive Gnocchi

At Frankie's, we serve this on our winter seasonal menu. Apparently there are a lot of olive lovers in Redmond because this is one of our best selling seasonal dishes. We've served it at times with linguine instead of gnocchi. Both are excellent choices. Bow-tie pasta would also be a great match.

At the restaurant we use three different types of olives; green olives, black olives and calamatas. For making this at home I suggest purchasing mixed olives from the deli section of the market.

Serves 6

1 recipe potato gnocchi (or one pound store bought gnocchi or pasta)

1/2 cup extra virgin olive oil

6--4 ounce boneless, skinless chicken breast--sliced crosswise

1 cup mixed olives--pitted and roughly chopped

1/3 cup sun-dried tomatoes

2 to 3 cloves garlic--chopped fine

5 ounces spinach--cleaned and roughly chopped

1/2 cup parmesan (preferably Parmigiano-Reggiano) - grated

4 ounces Feta cheese

Italian parsley for garnish (optional)

1. Bring 4 quarts water to boil in a large pot for cooking gnocchi. When boiling, add a tablesoon of salt.

2. Heat 2 tablespoon of the olive oil in a deep sauté pan over medium-high heat. Add the sliced chicken and sauté until nearly cooked through.

3. Add the olives, sun-dried tomatoes and garlic and cook for one to two minutes. Add spinach and cook until fully wilted. Turn off heat.

4. In batches, add gnocchi to water and cook until they rise to the surface. Remove with a slotted spoon and drain.

5. When all gnocchi are cooked, add to the pan with the chicken and other items.

6. Turn heat on medium and add remaining olive oil and grated parmesan. Toss together.

7. Platter and top with Feta cheese and garnish with parsley if desired.

Suggested Wine: *Falanghina*

It makes sense that this dish, which has some Greek influence, would pair well with a wine which also has Greek origins; that being a white wine from the region of Campania known as Falanghina. Falanghina is one of my favorite Italian white wines. This is a ful-bodied, full-flavored white with a great deal of personality.

Frankie's recommendation: *Feudi di San Gregorio "Falanghina"*

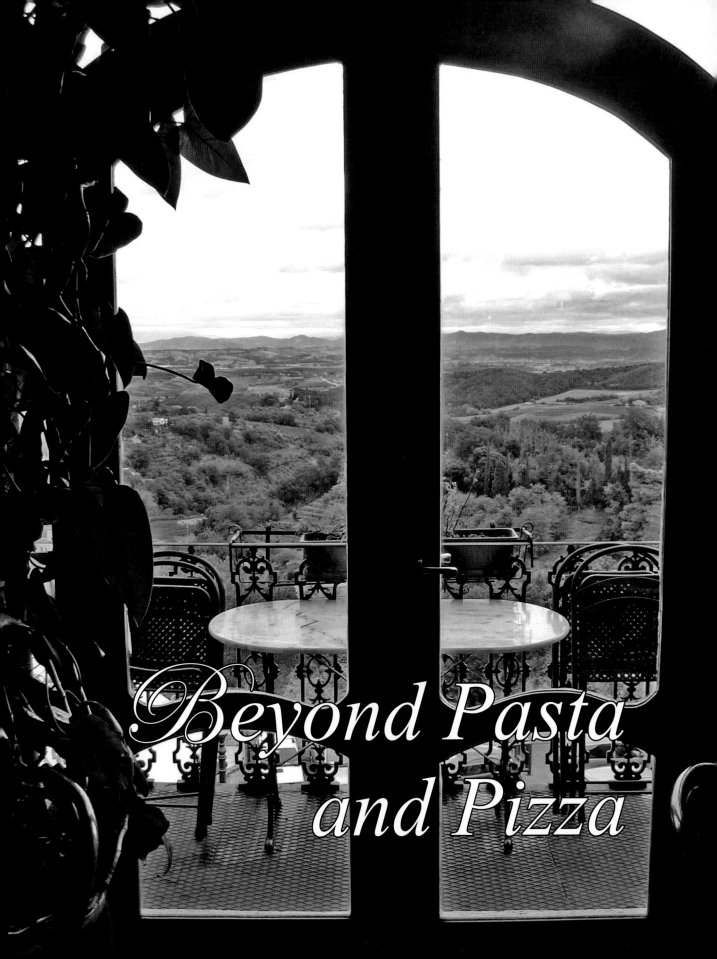

Beyond Pasta
and Pizza

Chicken Marsala

This dish is elegant and delicious, yet surprisingly easy to make. The sauce is made from sweet Marsala wine, a fortified dessert wine from the area surrounding the town of Marsala, Sicily.

There are many variations of this traditional recipe... some include onions, others mushrooms; some have chicken stock. I've tested numerous variations and customized this recipe to best suit the palate of my wife Rhonda and I. I believe it will tantalize your taste buds as well! You can also make this with veal if you desire. Serve this for a special dinner and your guests will think you're a culinary genius!

4 servings

4 boneless, skinless chicken breasts
5 to 6 oz. each (see Frankie's Tips)

3/4 cup all purpose flour

salt & pepper

2 tablespoons canola or vegetable oil

4 ounces pancetta (or thick-sliced un-smoked bacon)—diced in small pieces (1/4" or smaller)

6 ounces mushrooms—sliced thick

1 large shallot—minced

1 teaspoon tomato paste

1-1/2 cups sweet Marsala wine

1 tablespoon lemon juice

2 tablespoons Italian parsley—chopped

6 tablespoons butter--cut in 1 oz. pieces

1/2 teaspoon salt

****

1. Place oven rack in middle position; place an oven-proof platter on the oven rack. Heat oven to 200° F.

2. Trim excess fat from chicken. If thinner cutlets are desired, slice thinly or pound out with meat pounder (see Frankie's Tips). Pat the chicken dry and season both sides with salt and pepper.

3. Place flour in a shallow platter or baking dish. Working with one cutlet at a time, coat both sides with flour. Pat lightly with your hands to remove excess flour and place patties single layer on a platter.

4. Heat the oil in a large, flat-bottom skillet over medium-high heat until oil begins to shimmer. Place cutlets in a single layer in the skillet and cook until golden brown—2 to 3 minutes depending on thickness of chicken. Flip the cutlets with tongs, and cook an additional 2 to 4 minutes until firm to the touch when pressed (this indicates doneness). Transfer cutlets to the heated platter and place in oven to keep warm.

5. To prepare sauce, reduce heat to medium-low and add pancetta. Sauté, stirring occasionally with a large slotted spoon to loosen browned bits--until the pancetta is lightly crisped—about 4 to 5 minutes. Transfer pancetta with slotted spoon to a paper towel lined plate.

6. Increase the heat to medium-high and add mushrooms. Sauté, stirring minimally (flip over if necessary for even cooking), until mushrooms turn a beautiful golden brown—about 5 to 6 minutes.

7. Add minced shallot and cook and stir an additional 2 to 3 minutes, until softened. Add tomato paste and the cooked pancetta, and cook an additional minute.

8. Remove from heat while you add the Marsala. Return pan and increase heat to high. Simmer vigorously, scraping the browned bits from the pan bottom (this step is known as deglazing), until sauce reduces to somewhat of a syrupy consistency.

9. Turn off heat. Add lemon juice and Italian parsley. Whisk in butter, one tablespoon at a time. Add salt. Taste sauce and adjust seasoning if needed.

10. Remove chicken from oven. Place cutlets in sauce, along with any juices on the platter. Turn cutlets to coat lightly. Arrange on plates or platter and pour remaining sauce over the top.

Frankie's Tips:

- It's important to buy a good quality Marsala for this dish. There are some really cheap ones out there, some of which are produced in the USA, and not even true Marsalas

- You can use full-thickness chicken breasts with this entrée if desired but personally I like thinner cutlets. In many grocery stores you can purchase thinner cutlets (though you'll pay more). You can also accomplish this two other ways... the first is to slice the breasts thinner with a sharp knife to give you two thinner cutlets. The other is to pound out the meat with a meat pounder. If doing so, cover the meat with plastic wrap to avoid the juices flying around the kitchen.

- One sure way to ruin this dish is to overcook the chicken. The cooked chicken will be held in the 200° F oven for about 20 minutes while you prepare the sauce so it is best to under cook it just slightly prior to moving to the oven. You can go completely by feel if you are comfortable doing so or you can check the cutlets with an instant read thermometer for doneness. For safety, you want chicken to reach 165° F. Since they will continue to cook in the oven though, you should remove them from the pan when they have reached approximately 155° F.

Veal Parmigiana

This dish conjures up thoughts of dining in a charming old Italian family restaurant in little Italy. Maybe a few guys in fedoras speaking in hushed tones at the table next to us.

At Frankie's, we serve Chicken Parmesan. We've tried to serve veal, but there seems to be quite a few people who avoid it for reasons of conscience. If that describes you, chicken can easily be substituted. This would be wonderful served with a side of pasta with Marinara or Pink Sauce.

4 servings

8 - 2 ounce veal cutlets--pounded to 1/8 inch thickness (see Frankie's Tips)

salt (preferably Kosher or sea salt) and fresh ground black pepper

1/2 cup flour

3 eggs--beaten

1-1/4 cup dried bread crumbs (see instructions on page 147 if you'd like to make your own)

1 tablespoon dried oregano (or 2 tablespoons fresh)

approximately 1/2 cup olive oil

3 cups Marinara sauce

6 ounces provolone cheese--shredded (or sliced if you cannot find bulk)

3/4 cup freshly grated Parmigiano-Reggiano (lightly packed)

2 tablespoons fresh Italian parsley--chopped.

1. Set oven to broil and place rack in middle of oven.
2. Season cutlets lightly with salt and pepper.
3. Place flour, eggs and bread crumbs in three separate shallow dishes. Mix oregano into to bread crumbs.
4. Working with one cutlet at a time, dredge both sides in flour, dip into eggs, and then coat thoroughly with bread crumb mixture (press crumbs firmly against cutlet to help them adhere well). Transfer to baking sheet lined with parchment or butcher paper.
5. Pour olive oil into skillet to a depth of 1/8 inch or less. Warm over medium-high heat until oil is shimmering.
6. Cook two or three pieces of veal at a time, turning once with tongs, until golden-brown, about 3 minutes. Transfer to a baking sheet lined with foil.
7. Dump oil into a heat resistant container. Wipe out skillet with a wad of paper towels and add fresh oil. Repeat steps until all cutlets are cooked.
8. Top each cutlet with 1/4 cup of the marinara sauce.
9. If both cheeses are shredded or grated, mix them together. Place an equal amount atop each cutlet (note: if using sliced provolone cut or tear slices and place atop sauce, then top with parmigiano.
10. Broil until cheese is bubbly and lightly browned, about 5 minutes. Warm remaining Marinara and place on a platter. Place veal cutlets atop sauce. Top with chopped parsley.

Frankie's Tips:

♦ Having very thin cutlets, called scaloppine, is important for this Veal Parmigiano dish. Pounding them until they are very thin will tenderize the meat, and allow it to cook quickly and evenly. The trick is to accomplish this feat without tearing or damaging the meat.

♦ I really prefer a flat style meat pounder as shown in the photo (top right). It is much gentler on the meat and more effective in my experience. Pound cutlets using medium force. If the cutlets are long and narrow, pound from the middle outward to try a widen them. Take care not to work one part of the cutlet more than any other.

Suggested Wine: *Montepulciano d'Abruzzo*

Having a wine called Montepulciano from the region of Abruzzo, is confusing because there is a town in Tuscany with that name; and wines from that area also have the name Montepulciano in them (such as Vino Nobile de Montepulciano). In this case the name indicates the name of the grape, and Abruzzo is the region. Montepulciano wines from Abruzzo are known to be of excellent quality for the price.

Frankie's recommendation: *Farnese Montepulciano d'Abruzzo*

Eggplant Parmigiana

This Eggplant Parmesan recipe is different from most, in that it calls for baking the eggplant instead of coating and frying it prior to assembly, as most recipes call for. This both simplifies the preparation and makes it healthier. The results are delightful.

4-6 servings

2 globe eggplants (AKA American eggplants) minimum 1-1/2 lb. each--sliced 1/2 inch thick

1 teaspoon salt

1/3 cup olive oil

1-1/2 cups Marinara sauce

24 small fresh basil leaves—or larger leaves torn in pieces

1-3/4 cup shredded mozzarella (or fresh mozzarella—diced small)

1 cup freshly grated Parmigiano-Reggiano (lightly packed)

fresh ground black pepper

1. Preheat oven to 425 F. Generously brush two large baking sheets with olive oil. Place the eggplant slices on the trays in a single layer. Lightly brush the top side of the eggplants with the remaining oil. Lightly sprinkle with salt.

2. Bake in oven for 20 minutes until tender and lightly browned (if you need to place the trays on separate oven racks, switch the trays midway through the baking process). When eggplants are done baking, remove from oven and reduce oven to 400 F. Allow eggplant to rest until cool enough to handle.

3. While eggplants are baking and cooling, prep remaining ingredients.

4. Place 1/3 cup Marinara in bottom of an 11x13 baking dish.

5. Place 1/3 of your eggplant slices in a single layer atop the sauce. Place 1/3 cup Marinara atop the eggplant. Place 12 basil leaves atop the sauce. Top with 1/4 cup of Parmigiano and 1/2 cup of mozzarella.

6. For the second layer, repeat step 5.

7. For the top layer, place the final layer of eggplant and then grate fresh black pepper over that. Top with the remaining 1/2 cup of sauce, 1/2 cup of Parmigiano and 3/4 cup of mozzarella.

8. Cover baking dish with foil and bake for 20 minutes. Remove foil and bake an additional 10-12 minutes until cheese is bubbly and nicely browned.

9. Allow to rest ten minutes before slicing.

Suggested Wine: *Di Majo Norante "Ramitello"*

I simply listed the full name of the wine above because it is a unique blend of Prugnolo (a clone of Sangiovese) and Aglianico from the region of Molise; a tiny region in southern Italy. This wine may be a little tricky to find (though I'd be happy to sell it to you!). Sangiovese would be a reasonable alternative.

Frankie's recommendation: *Di Majo Norante "Ramitello"*

Frankie's Tips:

♦ Eggplant will soak up oil like a sponge. Brush lightly or the finished dish will be very oily.

♦ Many recipes call for salting eggplant and placing slices in a colander with a weighted plate on top to remove excess juices which they claim are bitter. I've tried this several times and have never gotten a drop of juice. Nor have I ever perceived my eggplant as being bitter. Personally I think it is a waste of time.

♦ One problem I have encountered though is tough skin on some eggplants, which is hard to cut through on the finished dish. In my experience, the older the eggplant, the more likely this will occur. If you notice the skin to be very tough when slicing, feel free to skin the eggplant. This will give you a more tender dish. I prefer mine with skin on though, and it is more nutritious as well.

♦ The amount of sauce in each layer looks skimpy. It is tempting to add more. I did so on my first test batch, and it was way too saucy. Also, notice that there is more sauce and cheese on your final layer. You want to cover the eggplant well for the best results when baking.

Pizza Rustica (AKA Torta Rustica)

This is not really a pizza in the traditional sense. Sometimes it is referred to as a torta. In Naples and other parts of southern Italy it is traditionally served on Ash Wednesday and again on Easter so it is also known as Easter Pie. It is very unique in that it combines a sweet, tender, egg pastry dough (what the Italians call pasta frolla) with savory fillings. The sweet-savory combination comes alive in your mouth. It is one of my personal favorites.

If you are having a party and don't mind going to a little trouble—this delightful, unusual dish will impress your guests like few others. It looks gorgeous. It's delicious. And it tastes unlike anything they've ever had before. We made it for one of our wine dinners and it was one of the most popular dishes we've ever served. It would also be a perfect brunch entrée. It may be served hot or at room temperature.

Serves 8-10

Pasta Frolla Ingredients:

2-1/2 cups all-purpose flour

1/4 cup sugar

1 teaspoon salt

1 teaspoon baking powder

10 tablespoons (1-1/4 sticks) butter—chilled—cut into small pieces

2 large eggs

Ice water

one 10 inch diameter x 2 inch deep cake pan *or* spring form pan—buttered

Filling Ingredients:

4 large eggs

1-1/2 pounds ricotta

12 ounces mozzarella—coarsely grated

1/2 cup Pecorino Romano—grated (or Parmigiano-Reggiano)

6 ounces prosciutto—diced

6 ounces salami (or other dried sausage) - diced

6 tablespoons fresh parsley—chopped

1/2 teaspoon fresh ground pepper

1/2 teaspoon salt

egg wash: 1 egg well beaten with 1 teaspoon water and pinch of salt

Preparing the Pasta Frolla:

1. Place flour, sugar, salt and baking powder in food processor fitted with metal blade. Pulse 3-4 times to mix.

2. Add chilled butter. Pulse until 6 or 7 times until it resembles coarse meal. Add eggs and continue pulsing until it just begins to form a ball (if needed—add ice water in tiny amounts until it begins to come together). Do not overwork.

3. Remove dough and press it together with your hands. Divide into two pieces, the larger of which is two-thirds of the dough. Form each part into a round disk. Cover with plastic wrap and chill for a minimum of 30 minutes. Note: It can also be made several hours ahead, or even the day before.

Preparing the filling:

1. Place ricotta in a strainer lined with a cheesecloth or paper towels and allow to drain for 15-20 minutes to remove excess liquid.

2. Place eggs in a bowl and beat briefly with a whisk. Add ricotta and whisk until mixture is creamy.

3. Add all remaining filling ingredients and mix thoroughly with a large spoon until well blended.

Finishing the Pizza Rustica:

1. Set rack in middle of oven and preheat to 350° F.

2. Place two sheets of plastic wrap, side by side and slightly overlapping, on a moist surface (to keep them from sliding around). Unwrap the large chilled dough and place atop plastic wrap. Cover with two more sheets of overlapping plastic wrap. Gently roll the covered dough into approximately a 16" circle.

Continued page 176

Pizza Rustica
(AKA Torta Rustica)

Suggested Wine: *Salice Salentino*

Salice Salentino hails from the region of Apulia, the heel of Italy's boot. It is made mostly from the Negroamaro grape which means *black and bitter* or *blackest of the black*. For this reason I'm was surprised at how well it goes with this dish which has a sweetness to it. It is likely because of the ripeness brought about by the southern Italian sun.

Frankie's recommendation: *Terre del Grico "Salice Salentino"*

Pizza Rustica variations:

This version of Pizza Rustica is a fairly typical example of the fillings used in Naples from where it originates. Many variations are common however, and like any pizza, only your imagination will limit the possibilities. You can either blend them in with other fillings or layer on top. Some fillings which I like include...

♦ Spinach—you can use fresh or frozen. The thing to watch our for is extra moisture. If using fresh, cook it briefly to sweat out the excess moisture, and squeeze dry with paper towels or cheesecloth. If using frozen, squeeze dry also—though there is no need to cook it first.

♦ Roasted red peppers—you can roast your own (see procedure on page 76), or buy them canned—in which case you would want to drain off excess moisture.

♦ Italian sausage—either spicy or mild—pre-cooked.

♦ Substitute any cured meat for the salami such as mortadella, pepperoni, or sopressata.

Finishing the Pizza Rustica:

3. Remove the top sheets of plastic wrap. Gently place the dough, plastic wrap up, into the cake pan. Remove plastic wrap. Press dough into the pan, leaving some overlapping the top rim.

    Note: It is very likely you will have some tearing of the pastry dough either during the transfer or when pressing it into the pan. Relax—this is easy to repair—simply press the dough together where it has torn and/or use excess dough to the repair holes.

4. Place the filling into the dough and smooth out the top. Cut off excess dough so that it extends about a half inch above the filling. Save the scraps—press together and wrap with plastic wrap.

5. Remove the smaller piece of dough and roll into approximately an 11-12 inch circle—using the method described above. Remove top layer of plastic wrap. Place the cake pan atop the dough and using a pairing knife—cut around the exterior of the pan to form a circular piece of dough for the top. Place atop filling. Save the remaining dough scraps with the others.

6. Fold the dough from the bottom crust over the edge of the top dough and gently press together to seal. With your pairing knife cut several vent holes in the top of the dough.

7. Form the scraps into a ball and roll out on a lightly flowered surface. Cut into decorative shapes. Brush top dough with egg wash. Place decorative shapes atop dough and brush these also.

8. Bake on middle rack 50 to 55 minutes until top is nicely browned.

9. Cool in the pan on a rack for a minimum of 10 minutes. To unmold, take a pairing knife and run it around the edge of the pan to loosen the pie. Put a plate over the top of the pizza and invert it. Then place a flat serving plate or platter upon the bottom and invert again. If you have used a spring form pan, simply remove the sides. You can either leave it on the bottom tray or invert twice as described above to remove the bottom.

10. Allow to cool an additional 5 to 10 minutes before slicing—or for a few hours if you desire to serve at room temperature. Use a sharp knife for slicing.

Frankie's Tips:

The filling for this pizza is easy to make. The dough is more complicated but the good news is it is a very forgiving dough—tears are easy to repair—and blemishes just add to it's rusticity. A few tips to help you...

♦   It's very important that the butter is chilled. Otherwise the dough will be too soft and not flaky.

♦   It is also important that your dough is chilled before you begin to roll it out.

♦   You do not want to overwork the dough, which will make it tough and hard to work with. That is why you only want to process the dough until it starts to come together. Finish forming by hand.

♦   Some recipes call for the top crust to be a lattice. I personally prefer a solid crust decorated with pastry shapes.

♦   One last tip—if you are inexperienced at rolling out dough, you will probably get frustrated at how the edges of the dough want to split. To begin with, go slow. Start by rolling gently from the center outwards, but then if it starts to split, push the split areas together and roll around the edges which will help it to come together. Deep breathing might help too!

Frankie's Timpano *(recipe on following page)*

Few American's had heard of *Timpano* until it was featured in the movie "Big Night". Those of you who have seen the movie will understand the "mystique" which surrounds it. Those who have not seen the movie... well what can I say other than you've missed one of the great cult "foodie" classics of all time (possibly my all time favorite movie). The story, set in the mid-fifties, portrays two brothers from Italy struggling to keep their failing New Jersey restaurant afloat. The food scenes alone are enough to make the movie worthwhile but it is also rich in Italian immigrant culture, life, and a sound track which can't be missed. Stanley Tucci, who had a hand in writing the movie, co-directs and stars along with Tony Shalhoub (of *Taxi* fame), Minnie Driver, Marc Anthony, and Isabella Rossellini among others.

As far as Timpano, it's a dish which Stanley Tucci's grandmother brought to America from Calabria, the toe of Italy's boot. It is traditionally made in a deep enamel drum-shaped pan--big enough to feed a small army (though there is a smaller size available). It has a pasta dough exterior and is filled with wonderful goodies such as pasta, meatballs, sausage, salami, eggs, cheeses and tomato sauce.

Suggested Wine: *Sicilia Rosso*

This wine, from one of Sicily's leading producers, is mostly indigenous Nero d'Avola with the addition of Merlot, Syrah and Cabernet Franc. The wine is supple, round and dry with medium to full body. Ripe, berry fruits with a chewy texture. Its good acidity and structure keep the wine balanced, and the finish long and clean.

Frankie's recommendation: *Planeta "La Segreta" Rosso*

Buying Timpano Pans:

There are several sources on-line for purchasing Timpano pans. My favorite is **FG Pizza & Italian** at **www.fgpizza.com.** They sell two sizes of Timpano pans (most places only sell the large), as well as other home pizza and pasta making equipment. They also sell the 00 flour which I discuss in the pizza making section. When I contacted the owner--who is also named Frankie--it turns out I knew him. He used to sell pepperoni and other foods.

Frankie's Timpano--the recipe

Serves 16-20

Pasta Dough:

4 cups all purpose flour

4 large eggs

1 teaspoon salt

2 tablespoons olive oil

up to 1/2 cup water

Timpano Filling:

2 pounds ziti (or penne) pasta--cooked 1/2 of the time listed on package

2 tablespoons extra virgin olive oil

1/4 cup fresh parsley—chopped

11 cups Sicilian Meat Sauce (recipe on page 100--you will need to double recipe)

1 recipe meatballs (recipe on page 102)--made smaller (20 to 24 meatballs)

12 hard-boiled eggs--shelled, quartered lengthwise, with each quarter cut in half

2 cups Genoa salami (or other dried sausage)--diced in 1/4 to 1/2 inch pieces

2-1/2 cups sharp provolone cheese--diced in 1/4 to 1/2 inch pieces

1 cup Pecorino Romano—grated

4 large eggs--beaten

1/2 pound peas (optional)

Pre-prep:

1. Prepare meatballs and sauce. Boil eggs, and cook pasta (half way). Set aside to cool. Note: You can prep the salami and cheeses after you make the pasta dough since the dough will need time to rest.

Preparing the Pasta Dough:

1. Place the flour, eggs, salt and olive oil in the bowl of a food processor fitted with a metal blade. Add 1/4 cup of the water. Process for 15 seconds.

2. Stop the processor and feel the dough. It should adhere together when squeezed between your fingers (but not feel too wet and sticky). If the mixture has not begun to form a ball, gradually add cold water, 1 tablespoon at a time, and continue to process in short intervals until the mixture just begins to come together as a ball.

3. Remove dough from processor and place on a lightly floured work surface. Knead with the ball of your hand, turning and folding several times, until the dough is smooth and elastic. Press into a circle about one inch thick. Place in a plastic bag, or wrap with plastic wrap, and set aside to rest for at least 15 to 20 minutes.

4. Flatten dough on a large, lightly floured work surface. Dust the dough with flour. Roll out the dough, working from the center outwards. Dust with additional flour and flip the dough over from time to time as needed, until it is the desired diameter (see Frankie's Tips).

5. Generously grease timpano pan with butter and olive oil. Fold the dough in half, and then in half again to form a triangle. Place in pan. Open dough and form into the pan, pressing gently against the bottom and sides, draping the extra dough over the sides.

Preparing the Timpano filling:

1. Preheat oven to 350° F.

2. Toss drained pasta with olive oil, parsley, and 3 cups of sauce. Distribute 4 cups of the pasta on the bottom of the Timpano pan.

3. Top with a bit less than half of each of the following: meatballs, hard-boiled eggs, salami, provolone, Pecorino, and peas.

4. Pour 1/4 of beaten eggs over top and spread around so it can soak down.

5. Pour 2 cups of sauce over these ingredients.

6. For the next layer, distribute 6 generous cups of the pasta.

7. Top with remaining meats, hard boiled eggs, cheeses and peas. Pour 1/3 of remaining beaten eggs over top and spread around.

8. Pour 3 cups of sauce over these ingredients.

9. Fill with additional pasta until the filling is about 3/4 inch from the rim of the pan (you may have a little pasta left over).

10. Pour remaining beaten eggs over top and spread around. Top with remaining sauce.

11. Fold pasta dough over filling to seal completely. Trim away excess dough. Brush lightly with olive oil.

12. Bake one hour until top is lightly browned. Then cover with foil and bake until the internal temperature reaches 120° F. (about 30 to 45 minutes more).

13. Remove from oven and rest for 30 minutes.

14. Place a large platter or cutting board on top of Timpano pan and carefully invert.

15. Drum roll please! Remove pan by twisting and lifting. Applause please!

16. Allow to cool an additional 10 to 15 minutes.

17. Using a long, narrow bladed knife, cut a circle, about 2 inches in diameter, in the center of the Timpano, being careful to cut all the way through to the bottom. Then slice the Timpano, as you would a pie, into individual portions, leaving the center circle as support.

18. Take a bow for your adoring fans!

Frankie's Tips:

♦ Note that you will need a total of 20 eggs, 12 of which are hard boiled.

♦ For making the dough, I have given instructions for the food processor method which I think is easiest. You can also make it in a stand mixer with a dough hook, or by hand on the counter top the way Stanley Tucci's grandmother would have made it. This takes a little practice.

♦ To roll out the dough, you need a rather large work surface because the dough for a large Timpano needs to be rolled out to at least 32 inches in diameter.

♦ The filling is essentially 5 layers, with layers of sauced pasta on the bottom, middle and top, and 2 layers of other fillings sandwiched in between.

♦ The peas are not a traditional filling but I like the flavor and moisture they add.

♦ You can use any oven proof bowl or pan for your Timpano. The traditional pans, which are enamel can be purchased on-line (see info on page 177). The large size is 14 inches in diameter. There is a smaller 10 inch pan which will feed 6 to 7 people. I did some volume measuring and determined it is 3/8 the size of the large pan. So if making a small pan, cut the dough recipe in half and do a bit less than half of all of the fillings. The smaller size bakes in just a little over an hour.

♦ You need to think ahead when making Timpano. The pre-preparation requires a lot of time. You can make the meatballs and sauce 2 to 3 days in advance which will make things easier. Once those are done you probably need a couple more hours to prep ingredients and at least 2-1/2 hours to bake and cool.

♦ Timpano can tend to be a little dry. I've increased the sauce, but any more causes it to not hold together. Consider serving additional sauce on the side.

Italian Ricotta Cheesecake

At Frankie's we serve a New York style cheesecake. It is dense and rich and sweet. Quite good actually—and popular with our guests. Personally though I adore this Italian-style cheesecake made with ricotta cheese. It is lighter and not so sweet. I highly recommend it with the sauce which can be made year round using frozen berries. This is worth having a party so you can share!

Serves 12

Crust:

1-3/4 cup graham cracker crumbs

1/2 cup sugar

6 tablespoons butter—melted, plus 1 tablespoon for buttering the pan

3/4 teaspoon almond extract

Filling:

2 pounds ricotta cheese

4 large eggs—separated

3/4 cup granulated sugar

1/4 cup Grand Marnier

1 tablespoon all-purpose flour

grated zest of one medium lemon

2 teaspoons vanilla extract

1/8 teaspoon salt

Berry Sauce (Frutta de Bosco):

1 pound (2 cups) fresh or frozen berries (such as blueberries, blackberries, raspberries or a blend thereof)

2 tablespoons granulated sugar

1 tablespoon balsamic vinegar

3/4 teaspoon corn starch

To prepare sauce—warm berries, sugar and balsamic vinegar in a medium sauce pan. Ladle some of the juices into a small bowl—cool for a minute and then whisk in cornstarch. Whisk this slurry into berry sauce. Bring to a simmer and then turn off heat and allow to cool. Cover and refrigerate.

1. Place the ricotta cheese in a fine-mesh sieve lined with cheesecloth or two layers of paper towels. Place the sieve atop a bowl and place in the refrigerator for at least 2 hours (preferably 3-4 hours or even overnight).

2. Place oven rack in middle position. Heat oven to 325° F.

3. Combine crust ingredients in a bowl and mix with your fingers (or a fork) until evenly moistened.

4. Brush the bottom and sides of a 9 inch spring form pan with most of the remaining tablespoon of melted butter. Place the crumb mixture into the spring form pan and with four fingers and fists, press mixture evenly over bottom and 3/4 inch up the side of the pan.

5. Bake until fragrant and beginning to brown—about 13 minutes. Cool pan on wire rack while preparing filling. Brush remaining butter on exposed interior of pan.

6. Place the drained ricotta in the work bowl of a food processor fitted with blade. Process until smooth, about 30 seconds.

7. Add the egg yolks (but not the whites!), along with sugar, Grand Marnier, flour, vanilla and salt—and process until well blended. Scrape mixture into a large bowl.

8. Using a mixer, beat the egg whites on high speed until they hold stiff peaks. Fold the egg whites into the ricotta mixture.

9. Bake cheesecake until the top is lightly browned and an instant-read thermometer inserted in middle reads approximately 150° F—about 1 hour and 20 minutes.

10. Transfer the pan to a wire rack and cool the cheesecake for 2 to 3 hours (until barely warm). Cover with two layers of plastic wrap and place in the refrigerator or freezer (see Frankie's Tips) for at least 6 hours.

11. Run a paring knife between the cake and the side of the pan. To unmold the pan, remove the sides. If you wish to transfer to a platter, use a large, flat spatula to gently loosen the cheesecake from the spring form bottom and gently transfer to the platter.

12. For clean cuts—fill a tall coffee cup or glass with very hot water. Dip knife into water for 5-10 seconds. Wipe knife with a paper towel and make a cut. Repeat.

Frankie's Tips:

♦ I recommend that you make this the day prior to serving and refrigerate or freeze it overnight—or at the very least, make it first thing in the morning to serve in the evening (in which case you would want to begin draining your ricotta the evening prior). You want it to be fully set and well chilled. You could even make this up to a week ahead and freeze.

♦ For the cleanest possible cuts, freeze your cheesecake, then sit out at room temperature for about 30 minutes prior to cutting. Make sure the water for dipping your knife in is extra hot. Re-dip the knife prior to each cut and then wipe the knife to remove water and residue. In my experience a thin bladed boning knife works best.

♦ If you fail to drain the ricotta as instructed, the cheesecake will come out slightly wet with less of the lush, creamy texture you desire. If rushed, you can compensate by adding a little more flour but adding too much will make your cheesecake taste a little bit gummy.

♦ I love the depth of flavor that the balsamic vinegar brings to the sauce, but if you have your doubts, start with a little less and adjust to taste.

♦ For the Grand Marnier, the amount you need is equal to one of those little tiny bottles.

2008 piemonte - italia

Cascinetta Vietti
moscato d'asti
denominazione di origine controllata e garantita
ALCOHOL 5.5% BY VOL. - WHITE WINE - 750 ML

Strawberries in Moscato

Talk about a simple, yet delicious dessert! I'll give this one the prize.

As I type this, it is a cold December day and I'm daydreaming about the warm July day when the idea for this popped into my head. It must have been an inspiration from God, because oh baby it is yummy!

Moscato d'Asti is a sweet, sparkling, low-alcohol wine from the area of Asti in Piedmont. It is made from the Moscato (Muscat) grape and is wonderful for an apéritif or a "not too sweet" dessert wine. Pour it over some fresh sliced strawberries and top with whipped cream and anybody will be impressed!

Serves 4

2 pints fresh strawberries

1 bottle Moscato d'Asti

1 cup of whipping cream

2 tablespoons powdered sugar

1. Chill glasses and the mixing bowl in which you will be whipping the cream.

2. Slice strawberries into halves or quarters. Reserve a nice one to use as a garnish for each serving. To prep the garnish berry, place it stem side down on a cutting board and slice into 5-6 slices, being careful not to slice all the way through to the stem. Fan out gently.

3. Whip the cream and powdered sugar until stiff. Be careful not to over whip and turn to butter.

4. Place strawberries in individual serving glasses and pour Moscato over the top (slowly so it does not fizz over).

5. Top with whipped cream and sliced strawberry.

6. Serve remaining Moscato on the side.

Frankie's Tips:

♦ If you like your whipped cream even a little richer and firmer, try adding some mascarpone cheese to it (that's what I did here). It makes a good thing taste even better.

♦ I left the traditional vanilla out of my whipped cream so as not to compete with the Moscato flavors.

♦ Personally I would only make this when strawberries are in peak season. Off-season strawberries lack so much in flavor. I really like the local northwest strawberries we enjoy in June and July.

♦ This would also be very delicious with fresh raspberries.

Grilled Peaches

This is one of my favorite summer desserts and very easy to prepare. Often I will grill them after I barbecue dinner, while the grill is still hot. Peaches are my favorite, but this is excellent with any stone fruit such as plums, apricots or nectarines.

Serves 4

4 ripe peaches (preferably freestone)

1/2 cup + 1 tablespoon honey

1/4 olive oil

2 tablespoons balsamic vinegar

1. Whisk together honey, oil and balsamic vinegar and pour into a baking dish.

2. Cut the peaches in half from pole to pole and remove pits. Place peaches cut side down in the honey glaze in the baking dish (this can be done an hour or more ahead if you desire).

3. Heat barbecue to medium-high heat. Scrape grill well before grilling peaches.

4. Place peaches on grill cut side down. Allow to grill 3 to 4 minutes until cut side begins to brown. With tongs, turn peaches over and grill an additional 3 to 4 minutes.

5. Brush on additional glaze. Turn cut side down again and grill until peaches are tender and cut side is caramelized.

Frankie's Tips:

♦ Serve with one of the following or use your own creativity…

• Vanilla gelato or ice cream

• Whipped cream or mascarpone cream*

♦ If you want to make it even better, consider one of the following garnishes…

• Fresh raspberries or blackberries (or raspberry freezer jam)

• Crushed Amaretti cookies (Italian almond flavored cookies)

* To make Mascarpone Whipped Cream—in a chilled mixing bowl, beat together 8 ounces of room temperature mascarpone cheese with 2 cups heavy whipping cream and 1/4 cup sugar—until soft, fluffy peaks form; about 1 to 2 minutes. Cover and refrigerate for up to 30 minutes.

Our granddaughter Teddy enjoying the fruits of our labor.

Fresh Berry-Mascarpone Tart

Is there anything more delicious than summer berries at their peak? Of all summer's bounty, they win the grand prize in my book. This tart can be made with any fresh summer berries: raspberries, strawberries, blueberries, blackberries, or even a combination.

And if you've never made a tart shell before, don't be intimidated. This tart dough recipe is very simple, and can be made in the food processor; or you can buy some frozen pie dough and use that instead.

Mascarpone, if you are not familiar with it, is a rich, creamy Italian cheese, which is similar to cream cheese, only richer and more buttery in character. For this recipe we've blended it with whipping cream and powdered sugar and placed that in the pre-baked tart shell as a base for the berries.

Serves 6-8

Tart Dough Recipe:

1 cup + 1 tablespoon all purpose flour

1-1/2 tablespoons sugar

1/4 teaspoon salt

1/4 pound chilled butter—cut into 8 pieces

1 egg yolk

2 tablespoons ice water

Berry Glaze and Filling:

3 cups fresh berries (2-1/2 cups + 1/2 cup to create the glaze)

1/2 cup sugar

1/4 cup water

1 tablespoon lemon juice

1 tablespoon cornstarch

2 tablespoons water

Mascarpone Cream:

1 cup mascarpone cheese—bring to room temperature

1/2 cup whipping cream

3/4 cup powdered sugar

Equipment Needed:

food processor

rolling pin

9" tart pan (with removable bottom)

mixer (stand mixer or hand held)

Tart dough procedure:

1. Place the flour, sugar and butter in food processor. Process quickly until it resembles coarse meal or tiny peas. Add the egg yolk and ice water through the funnel. Process until the dough forms a ball around the blade.

2. On a floured surface, form the ball into a disk (about an inch thick). Cover with plastic wrap and place in the refrigerator for at least 20 minutes.

3. Preheat oven to 425 F.

4. Place dough on a floured surface. Flour roller and roll out dough to a 12" circle. Fold in quarters and transfer to the tart pan. Press the dough into pan with your fingers, trying to make it roughly the same thickness throughout. Take your roller and roll it across the top of the tart pan to cut off the edges. If you have any thin spots, use this excess dough to patch.

5. Prick the bottom with a fork and bake un-filled for 12 minutes (see Frankie's Tips for option). Cool in pan. Do not remove from tart pan until you are ready to serve the tart.

Preparing Berry Glaze and Filling:

1. To make the glaze which will coat the remaining berries, place 1/2 cup of the berries into a small sauce pan. Add sugar and 1/4 cup water and cook over medium heat until simmering. Using a potato masher, smash the berries (the smoother the better).

2. In a small bowl, whisk together the lemon juice, cornstarch and 2 tablespoons water. Spoon a couple of tablespoons of the hot berry liquid into the lemon juice-cornstarch mixture and whisk.

3. Reduce heat to low and whisk the lemon juice-cornstarch mixture into the berry mixture. Cook until well blended and thickened to a thin jelly like consistency (if too thick, whisk in a little more water).

4. Place remaining berries in a bowl. After berry glaze has cooled to room temperature, stir gently into the berries to coat evenly.

Preparing Mascarpone Cream: (can be prepared while berry glaze is cooling)

1. Place mascarpone in mixing bowl. Mix on high speed until smooth and lump free.

2. Add cream and powdered sugar and mix for one minute. Spread in bottom of cooled tart shell.

3. Top with berry filling and refrigerate until ready to serve.

Frankie's Tips:

♦ If you would like to simplify things you can use berry jelly or preserves to glaze the berries. You'd likely need to warm and thin slightly with water.

♦ One problem with baking an empty tart shell is it tends to shrink down slightly. To better maintain the integrity of the shell you can fill the crust with pastry dough weights (available at kitchen supply stores) or fill the shell with beans or barley prior to baking. If you use one of these, add one minute to baking time.

Rustic Grape Crostata

I had decided to make this because I had such an abundant harvest of grapes last year, and did not want them to go bad before we had a chance to eat them all. It was delicious! I used blue grapes, but you could use seedless red, blue or black grapes; or a blend of two or three depending on availability. Just make sure the grapes are juicy for the best results.

Serves 8

Pastry Dough:

1 cup all–purpose flour

1/4 cup yellow cornmeal

3 tablespoons granulated sugar

1/2 teaspoon baking powder

1/2 teaspoon salt

1/4 cup chilled butter—cut into 1/2 inch pieces

3 tablespoons orange juice

1 teaspoon all–purpose flour

Filling:

5 cups seedless grapes (see intro) - stems removed

3 tablespoons granulated sugar

1 tablespoon cornstarch

1 teaspoon vanilla extract

1/4 teaspoon ground cinnamon

For top of tart:

1 teaspoon water

1 egg yolk

1 teaspoon turbinado sugar

****

Preparing the pastry Dough:

1. Preheat oven to 400º F. Place parchment paper or a Silpat baking mat on a baking sheet.

2. Combine the flour, cornmeal, 3 tablespoons granulated sugar, baking powder and salt in the bowl of a food processor. Pulse 3-4 times to blend.

3. Add chilled butter. Pulse 6 or 7 times until it resembles coarse meal. With processor running, slowly pour orange juice through food chute, processing until it just starts to come together (do not allow dough to form a ball at this point).

4. Remove dough and press it together with your hands to form a 4 to 5 inch disk. Cover with plastic wrap and chill for a minimum of 15 minutes.

Preparing the filling:

1. Place 1 cup of grapes in a blender or food processor along with the 3 tablespoons of granulated sugar. Process briefly until relatively smooth.

2. Transfer to a large sauce pan. If the grapes lack juiciness, add a couple of tablespoons of water. Whisk in the cornstarch, vanilla extract and cinnamon.

3. Heat over medium heat until grape mixture comes to a simmer. Reduce heat and simmer two minutes. Remove from heat. Fold in remaining grapes and cool.

Finishing the crostata:

1. Slightly overlap two sheets of plastic wrap, on a moist surface (to keep them from sliding around). Unwrap the chilled dough and place atop plastic wrap. Cover with two more sheets of overlapping plastic wrap. Gently roll the covered dough into a 12" circle. Remove the top sheets of plastic wrap and place dough, plastic wrap up on the lined baking sheet. Remove remaining plastic wrap. Sprinkle with one teaspoon of flour.

2. Spoon cooled grape mixture into center of dough, leaving the outer 2-3 inches with no topping. Fold the edges of the dough toward the center, over-lapping sections as you work your way around.

3. Combine the teaspoon of water with egg yolk. Brush over edges of dough. Sprinkle turbinado sugar over grape mixture and dough.

4. Bake for 25 minutes or until crust is golden brown. Serve warm or at room temperature with whipped cream, ice cream or gelato.

5. Be prepared for a taste explosion. Buon appetito!

Frankie's Tips:

- ◆ Pastry dough tips: For those of you who've never made pastry dough, let me give you a few tips....

  - It is very important that the butter is chilled. Otherwise the dough will be too soft and not flaky.

  - It is also important that your dough is chilled before you begin to roll it out.

  - You do not want to overwork the dough, which will make it tough and hard to work with. That is why you only want to process the dough until it starts to come together. Finish forming by hand.

  - Also, the more liquid you add to a pastry dough, the more it will shrink up during baking. Therefore, you want just enough liquid to make the dough workable.

  - One last tip—if you are inexperienced at rolling out dough, you will probably get frustrated at how the edges of the dough want to split. Take your time. Start by rolling gently from the center outwards, but then if it starts to split, push the split areas together and roll around the edges which will help it come together. This is a rustic tart so don't worry about some frayed edges.

- ◆ This recipe has you creating a sauce by processing some of the grapes with sugar, to be tossed with the whole grapes. You could simplify this by using a half cup of grape jelly and reduce the quantity of fruit in the recipe to 4 cups. If you do, no cornstarch will be needed, but you would still want to add the cinnamon and vanilla.

- ◆ What is the best thickener? There are many alternatives to cornstarch and many opinions on which is best. Someone suggested quick-cooking (pearl) Tapioca, but I understand that it is not good with open fruit pies because it remains hard on top when exposed to oven heat. Potato flour is an excellent alternative. If you use it though, it should not be allowed to boil. Flour may also be used. You would need to use twice as much as (two tablespoons in this recipe).

Lemon Semifreddo

Semifreddo, which translates "half-cold", is a rich and creamy, semi-frozen dessert reminiscent of a frozen mousse. Originally from the north-central region of Emilia-Romagna, it has become popular throughout Italy. Though made with heavy cream and egg yolks, the lemon zest and juice in this gives it a light and refreshing character. We served this at a recent wine dinner where it was a huge hit!

Serves 10

1-1/4 cup sugar

10 large egg yolks

zest of one medium lemon

1/2 cup fresh squeezed lemon juice

1/4 cup Limoncello (optional)

Pinch of salt

2 cups heavy cream

2 ounces amaretti cookies—crumbled for garnish (or lemon or vanilla wafers if you cannot find amaretti)

1. Spray a 9x5 inch loaf pan with non-stick cooking spray. Line the pan with plastic wrap, allowing enough to hang over the sides with which to cover the top after filling pan.

2. In order to create a double-boiler, place an inch of water in a large sauce pan. Bring to a simmer over low heat.

3. Place the sugar, egg yolks, lemon zest, lemon juice, limoncello, and salt in a large metal mixing bowl.

4. Place the bowl atop simmering water. Using a whisk or hand mixer, whisk the egg mixture until thick and creamy; and a thermometer inserted into the mixture registers 160° F (about 5-7 minutes). Set the bowl of custard into a bowl of ice water to cool completely.

5. In another large bowl, using an electric mixer, beat the heavy cream until peaks form. Gently fold the whipped cream into the custard using a large rubber spatula.

6. Spoon the mixture into the loaf pan. Cover with the overhanging plastic wrap and freeze until fully hardened (a minimum of 8 hours or up to 3 days).

7. When ready to serve, unfold the plastic wrap and using the wrap like handles, lift the semifreddo out of the pan and invert onto a platter (if it does not want to come out, dip the pan briefly in warm water).

8. Gently peel off the plastic wrap. Cut into 10 slices. Garnish with crumbled cookies, and serve.

9. Sit back and enjoy, and soak up the praises which will be heaped upon you. You deserve it!

Frankie's Tips:

♦ The idea of whisking the egg yolks over simmering water is to produce a light, airy custard—but also to ensure the raw eggs are safe for consumption. It is critical that you cool this thoroughly before mixing with the whipped cream.

♦ An delicious option with this semifreddo is the addition of pistachios nuts. If you desire to add these, roast 1/2 cup in a 350° F oven for 15 minutes. Cool completely and chop.

♦ Consider serving with Limoncello which compliments this dessert perfectly.

In 2008, we arrived in Monterosso, Cinque Terre just in time for their annual Lemon Festival. My wife Rhonda is the gorgeous babe on the right.

Tiramisu

Tiramisu means pick me up in Italian, in reference to the espresso or strong coffee used in it's preparation. It is an un-baked dessert, relying upon the ladyfingers, dipped in espresso, to give it its cake-like body. These are layered with zabaglione (pronounced za bal YOH nay), an egg yolk custard, mixed with mascarpone cheese. Most recipes also have some sort of liquor mixed with the coffee. We use Marsala.

My recipe has one thing which differentiates it from a traditional recipe, and that is the addition of a layer of raspberry sauce. I wanted ours to be original, and I love the combination of raspberry and chocolate so much that I tried it in this recipe and absolutely adored it. Some of my customers who are "purists" turn their nose up at it, but I've been told by countless others that this is the best Tiramisu they've ever had.

Makes one 9x13 dish
Serves 12-15

Raspberry Sauce:

2 tablespoon orange or lemon juice

1 tablespoon cornstarch

10 ounce package frozen raspberries

1/4 cup sugar

Flavored Coffee Dip:

3 cups strong coffee or espresso

1/2 cup Marsala wine

Zabaglione Mixture:

9 egg yolks

1-1/2 cups sugar

3/4 teaspoon orange zest

1/2 teaspoon vanilla

1-1/2 pounds (3 - 8 ounce containers) Mascarpone cheese

4 oz. cream cheese (room temperature)

Other Ingredients:

60 Ladyfingers (see Frankie's Tips)

2 ounces unsweetened cocoa

3 ounces dark chocolate shavings (optional--see Frankie's Tips)

Prepare Raspberry Puree:

1. Whisk juice and corn starch in a sauce pan. Place over medium heat. Add raspberries and sugar. Mash and stir until simmering and berries are well broken up. Cool.

Prepare Flavored Coffee Dip:

1. Measure strong coffee into a measuring cup. Place in a shallow baking dish or shallow pan. Add Marsala.

Prepare Zabaglione-Mascarpone Mixture:

1. Place egg yolks, sugar, orange zest and vanilla in a large stainless steel mixing bowl.

2. Create a double boiler by placing one inch of water in a large pot. Place over medium-high heat. Place mixing bowl on top.

3. Beat with a hand held electric mixer on high speed until the mixture has doubled in volume and has a pale color and a smooth, firm consistency. Mixture should reach 160 degrees and be really thick. Remove from heat and allow to cool. Continue the rest of process when mix has cooled below 90 F. (lukewarm or cool to touch).

4. Blend in mascarpone and cream cheese with mixer.

Assemble Tiramisu:

1. Briefly dip ladyfingers (both sides) into flavored coffee (one-at-a-time) and layer in bottom of baking dish, creating two rows of 8 to 10 (see Frankie's Tips).

2. Spread 1/3 of Zabaglione mixture over the ladyfingers.

3. Sprinkle a thin layer of cocoa over the entire Tiramisu.

4. Repeat steps 1 and 2. Then spread 1 cup of raspberry sauce on top of the second layer. Sprinkle a thin coating of cocoa on top of the raspberry.

5. Repeat steps one through three for your third layer. Do not put any Raspberry puree on the top layer.

Frankie's Tips:

♦ Shopping Tip: The trickiest part of this recipe is telling you how many ladyfingers to buy because they come in various sizes and pack quantities. If they are 12 ounce packs, you will probably need three. If they are 500 ml packages (over a pound), two will be adequate.

♦ This recipe for raspberry sauce will give you more than you need, but you won't have any problem using the leftovers. I promise! You can also use fresh raspberries of course.

♦ Espresso is traditional for dipping, but a very strong coffee is fine.

♦ Many different liquors are used in various recipes: brandy, vin santo, coffee liqueur. Any are okay. Marsala is a fortified wine from Sicily and generally inexpensive. A moderately priced brand is fine.

♦ The idea of whisking the egg yolks over simmering water is to produce a light, airy custard—but also to ensure the raw eggs are safe for consumption. It is important that you cool this thoroughly before mixing with the mascarpone and cream cheese.

♦ One of the trickiest parts is the dipping of the ladyfingers in the coffee. You want to be quick about it or they will soak up too much and become soggy (but if you are too quick they will be dry). Dip briefly, flip over and remove. If you are ambidexterous, you can do two at a time.

♦ The easiest way to sprinkle the cocoa is to put it in a shaker, if you have an extra one handy. If not, a fine mesh strainer will work, or just use your fingers. You just want a thin, even layer.

♦ A nice finishing garnish is to take a dark chocolate bar, and using a vegetable peeler on its edge, shave curls on top of the timamisu.

♦ For serving, you can either dip the tiramisu out with a spoon (traditional), or if you want nice individual cake-like portions, freeze it and then sit out at room temperature for 20 to 30 minutes prior to cutting. To cut, dip your knife in hot water and wipe clean before each cut. In my experience a thin bladed boning knife works best.

Orange-Hazelnut Biscotti

Homemade biscotti dipped in coffee or milk are one of life's great pleasures. A number of years ago my daughter-in-law, Sandra, began making the biscotti for our restaurant. What a treat! She makes dozens of variations and they are the best I've had anywhere. This orange-hazelnut is one of my favorites. I've also listed several yummy variations. If you apply a little imagination, I'm sure you can think of many more.

Makes 12 ~ 16 biscotti

1 cup hazelnuts—toasted and coarsely chopped

1/2 cup of butter (at room temperature)

1 cup sugar

1 tablespoon orange zest (about one large or tow medium oranges)

2 large eggs

1 teaspoon vanilla

2-1/2 cup all purpose flour

1 tablespoon baking powder

½ teaspoon salt

4 ounces semi-sweet chocolate (optional), or white chocolate, or both

1. Preheat oven to 350º F.

2. To toast hazelnuts, place on a baking sheet and place in oven for about 12 to 14 minutes until you get a fragrant, toasty aroma. Roughly chop after cooling.

3. On medium speed, beat together the butter, sugar, and orange zest. Add eggs, one at a time, beating well after each addition. Add in the vanilla.

4. In a separate bowl, combine flour, baking powder and salt. Add to the butter mixture a little at a time and blend thoroughly. Mix in cooled nuts.

5. Line a baking sheet pan with a Silpat pan liner, or parchment paper dusted with flour. Press the dough together and divide into two equal parts. Lightly flour each piece and shape into logs about 3 inches in diameter and 6 to 8 inches long. Press each log to make a 3/4 inch thick rectangle. It should be a little thicker in the middle down the length of the piece.

6. Bake until lightly browned, about 25 minutes. Cool for 10 minutes, and then slide gently onto a cutting board.

7. Using a long, sharp knife, cut each log crosswise into 3/4 inch thick slices.

8. Place cookies cut side down (on their side), back onto baking sheet. Bake cookies for 6 minutes; then flip the biscotti over and bake 7 minutes more. Allow to cool.

9. Melt chocolate (see Frankie's Tips). Drizzle melted chocolate over the biscotti.

Frankie's Tips:

♦ When the dough is being mixed it will not likely form into a ball. That's okay. When you pull it out of the mixing bowl, just press it together to form the logs.

♦ There are a variety of ways to melt chocolate. The two most common being a microwave (on half power) or creating a double boiler by placing a stainless steel or glass bowl atop a pan of simmering water. I find that white chocolate does not melt well in a microwave. I would only use the double boiler for that. Once melted you can either drizzle the chocolate with a spoon or place in a zip lock bag and cut a tiny hole in the corner; then squeeze over top of the biscotti.

ℬ*iscotti variations:*

One common biscotti flavoring the Italians use is anise seed, which has a slight licorice flavor. Personally it's not one of my favorites. But the number of other variations are nearly endless.

To modify this recipe, just take out the hazelnuts and orange zest and add the ingredients listed below. Chocolate or white chocolate is always an option. If using both dried fruits and nuts, I would use about 3/4 cup of each (vary to your liking). For zest, use about a tablespoon. Pretty much any dried fruit or citrus zest works well, as does just about any variety of nuts.

When doing the chocolate, you can also apply some variations such as dipping the bottom of the biscotti in the chocolate or dipping one end into it (in either of those cases you would need to use more chocolate).

Here are a few other ideas just to get your imagination stirring.

Dried Cherries, Chocolate & Pecans

Almonds & dried Figs

Pine Nuts & Lemon Zest

Macadamia Nuts & dried Pineapple (maybe with Coconut too?)

Dried Cranberries, Orange Zest, Walnuts & White Chocolate

Ricotta Fritters

I had always wanted to make these, and so I tested some variations for our staff Christmas party and they were a huge hit.

These are somewhat like a doughnut in that the batter is fried in oil. The major difference is they have ricotta cheese in them which makes them so airy and light. They are really quite easy to make and eating them warm and fresh is an experience you may never forget.

Makes about 35 fritters

1-1/2 cups all-purpose flour

1 tablespoon baking powder

3/4 teaspoon salt

4 eggs--room temperature-- lightly beaten

6 tablespoons honey

1 pound ricotta cheese (preferably whole milk)

2 teaspoons pure vanilla extract

zest of 2 lemons

2 tablespoon lemon juice

vegetable or canola oil for frying

confectioner's (powdered) sugar-- for dusting

lemon curls from one lemon for garnish (optional)

1. Whisk together dry ingredients (flour salt and baking powder).

2. Whisk together eggs, honey, ricotta, vanilla, lemon zest and lemon juice. Then whisk in flour mixture.

3. Heat 1-1/2 inches oil in a large wide heavy saucepan until the temperature is about 360° - 370° F.

4. Working in batches, gently drop batter into the hot oil, one tablespoon at a time, pushing the batter off the spoon with the rounded corner of a rubber spatula.

5. Batter will puff up immediately. Fry fritters, turning occasionally with a slotted spoon, until a deep golden brown, about 2 to 3 minutes per batch.

6. Using slotted spoon, transfer fritters to a tray lined with paper towels.

7. Dust generously with confectioners sugar. Garnish with zested curls of lemon peel if desired and serve warm.

Frankie's Tips:

♦ There are a number variations you can make with this. You can substitute orange zest and orange juice for the lemon; or instead of orange juice you can add Grand Marnier, which is an orange flavored liqueur. Some common additions to this include raisins or chocolate chips.

♦ It is important that you do not fry too many of these at a time because you will find it hard to cook them all evenly and you will cool the oil down too much. Start with just 3 or 4. As you get more comfortable you can try a 5 or 6 at a time.

♦ I recommend using a deep-fat thermometer to help you maintain the temperature. If you do not have one, but do have a stem thermometer, stop periodically and check temperature and adjust heat as needed.

Panforte

Panforte is a traditional dessert--really more of a gooey confectionery-originating from the ancient city of Siena many centuries ago, but now popular all over Italy. Though sometimes called an Italian fruitcake, it shares little resemblance to the version of fruit cake so many of you despise. Panforte's main ingredients are honey, sugar, almonds, hazelnuts, candied citrus peel. Some versions have dried fruits. It also has many of the spices you would find in a traditional spice cake. I made this for the holidays. Its so rich that its hard to eat a lot at once, but I couldn't keep from snacking on it several times per day.

A fun option is to make a number of mini Panforte to give away as gifts. To do so, double the recipe and cook in a 9x13 baking pan. Then using an oiled circular cutter, cut into mini Panforte's. Wrap each in wax paper and tie with colored string. You then have all the yummy leftover scraps to eat yourself.

One 9 to 10 inch Panforte - enough to feed 20 to 24

1 cup candied orange peel
(see Frankie's Tips)

2 cups blanched almonds--toasted and coarsely chopped (see Frankie's Tips)

2 cups hazelnuts--toasted and coarsely chopped

zest from two medium lemons

1 cup flour

1 tablespoon Dutch process cocoa powder

1 teaspoon salt

2 teaspoons cinnamon

1-1/4 teaspoon allspice

1-1/2 cup sugar

1-3/4 cup honey

6 ounces dried figs--diced (optional)

6 ounces dried apricots--diced (optional)

Confectioner's (powdered) sugar-- for dusting

1. If preparing your own candied orange peel, see procedure on page 205.

2. Preheat oven to 325° F. Place rack in center of oven.

3. Generously spray a 9 to 10 inch cake pan or spring-form pan (my choice) with nonstick cooking spray. Line bottom of pan with a parchment paper circle cut to fit. Spray parchment paper with nonstick spray also.

4. To toast almonds and hazelnuts, place on baking sheet and place in oven for 14 to 15 minutes until you get a fragrant, toasty aroma. Roughly chop after cooling.

5. Place chopped nuts in a large bowl with the lemon zest and candied orange peel. Toss to combine.

6. In another bowl, sift flour with cocoa powder and spices. Add to bowl of nuts. Toss until well combined. Set aside.

7. Mix sugar and honey in a large saucepan. Cook over low-medium heat, stirring occasionally to prevent scorching, until mixture comes to a full boil.

8. Remove pan from heat, and working very quickly, add the fruit and nut mixture. Stir thoroughly with a large spoon or heat resistant spatula. Scrape batter into prepared pan. Smooth top with slightly wet palm of hand or a wet spoon.

9. Bake panforte until it just begins to simmer around edge of pan, about 15 to 20 minutes.

10. Remove from oven and place pan on a wire rack to cool. To loosen panforte, run a small paring knife around perimeter of pan. Invert pan to remove panforte (or remove sides if using a spring form pan and then invert). Use paring knife to peel away parchment paper.

11. Invert right side up on wire rack. When fully cooled, dust generously with confectioner's sugar. Transfer to serving platter. Cut into narrow wedges (see Frankie's Tips).

Frankie's Tips:

- It is traditional in this recipe to use blanched almonds, which removes their skins. It's not easy to find them already blanched in a grocery store. In my opinion, it is not critical to the final product. But if you are a purist, you can blanch them by placing in a bowl and pouring boiling hot water over them. Allow to sit for one minute, then pour off the boiling water and immediately rinse with cool water. You can then slip the skins off one at a time, but beware, they are slippery. Once blanched, the nuts will be dried out in the roasting process. It is not critical to skin the hazelnuts.

- Candied orange peel is another item which may be difficult to find in your local grocery store (but can find them on-line quite easily). They are not too difficult to make yourself, but they do take a while to cook. See recipe on page 205. For the quantity you need here you would need about 2 medium oranges.

- If you have a rack full of spices but no allspice, you may substitute a combination of 1/2 teaspoon nutmeg, 1/2 teaspoon ground cloves and 1/4 teaspoon coriander.

- Be prepared to work very quickly once you add the other ingredients to the sugar-honey mixture. It will begin to harden pretty quickly as it cools down!

- To cut cleanly, dip your knife in hot water and wipe clean before each cut. In my experience a thin bladed knife, such as a boning knife, works best.

- I've had this with and without the dried apricots and figs and I prefer it with those added. Feel free to omit them though, or to add other dried fruits which are more to your liking.

Profiteroles
With Mocha Ice Cream filling

The history of profiteroles goes back several centuries, and though they are thought to be of French origin, you will find them in pastry shops throughout Italy. Profiteroles are made from a *choux* pastry dough and bear a similarity to cream puffs. Though often filled with pastry cream or whipped cream, ice cream is also common. They may look complicated, but they are actually quite easy. And whomever you make them for will think that you are a genius!

Makes 8 to 10 Profiteroles

Choux Pastry Dough:

3/4 cup water

1/4 cup milk

1/4 pound (1 stick) unsalted butter

1/8 teaspoon salt

1 cups all purpose flour

4 large eggs

Chocolate Mocha Sauce:

6 ounces semi-sweet chocolate

2 tablespoons honey

2 tablespoon espresso or strong coffee

1/4 cup whole milk or half & half

Filling:

one quart Mocha Ice cream

Equipment Needed:

aluminum baking tray

Silpat or parchment paper (optional)

large sauce pan

rubber spatula, wooden spoon and a whisk

pastry bag with 1/2 inch plain tip

mixer (preferably with mixing paddle)

medium sauce pan with a stainless steel bowl (for melting the chocolate)

Prepare Choux Pastry Dough:

1. Slowly heat water, milk, butter and salt to rolling boil in saucepan. Turn off heat. Add flour and stir vigorously with a wooden spoon until mixture forms a ball.

2. Transfer to mixing bowl fitted with paddle mixer. Allow to cool for 6 to 8 minutes before adding eggs.

3. Pre-heat oven to 425º F. Line baking tray with Silpat pad or parchment paper (or lightly butter and flour baking pan).

4. Add the eggs, one at a time and beat on slow speed, scraping sides of bowl periodically. Check consistency. Mixture should fall reluctantly from spoon (see Frankie's Tips).

5. Use a rubber spatula to scoop dough into pastry bag. Pipe in mounds, 2 to 2-1/2 inches wide and an inch thick, onto baking pan. Then make a second, slightly smaller mound on top of each until all Choux pastry is used up.

6. Bake for 15 minutes at 425º F. Reduce oven temperature to 350º and bake an additional 15 minutes.

7. Cool for a few minutes. Then, using a fork, separate the tops and place both halves, cut-side up on the tray. Return to oven for three minutes. Remove and cool. If any filaments of soft dough remain, remove with a fork.

Chocolate Mocha Sauce and final assembly:

1. Place one inch of water in a sauce pan over high heat until it begins to simmer. Reduce to low-medium heat.

2. Place first three Chocolate Mocha Sauce ingredients (except milk) in stainless bowl and place on top of simmering pot. Cover with plastic wrap until chocolate begins to melt and then stir with a whisk. Microwave milk for 20 seconds and add to chocolate. Whisk to achieve a smooth, pourable consistency (if too thick – add a little more hot milk). Spoon over top of Profiteroles. Allow time to set up.

3. You can freeze Profiteroles (with or without the chocolate sauce on them), for a few hours or a few days if desired. Bring out 30 minutes before serving. Fill each with a flattened scoops of ice cream.

Frankie's Tips:

♦ Dough needs to cool to lukewarm before you add eggs. If you'd like to speed the cooling process, turn the mixer on low for 4 to 5 minutes.

♦ Nothing worse than biting into an egg shell when enjoying your profiterole. I recommend that you crack your eggs into a bowl prior to adding to the choux pastry dough. This will allow you to check for eggs shells.

♦ If you happen to use extra large or jumbo eggs, check the consistency after adding 3 eggs (see step 4). Three jumbo eggs may be enough. If using extra large, you will probably need 3 eggs plus one egg white.

♦ Transfering choux pastry to a pastry piping bag can be a pain. Try putting you piping bag in a large pitcher or measuring cup, draping the sides over the side of the pitcher.

♦ When piping profiteroles onto baking tray, allow 2 to 3 inches between each to allow for rising.

Sicilian Cannoli

Cannoli is Italian for 'little tube' which describes what this dessert is; crisp, fried pastry shells embracing a creamy, sweet cheese filling. This delightful and fun dessert originates from Sicily. It is very popular throughout southern Italy as well as on the East Coast of the United States. We only occasionally sell them in the restaurant because many people out west are not familiar with them. That is a pity!

You can go two routes here. The first, and by far the simplest, is to purchase cannoli shells and then make the filling yourself. The shells can be found in Italian specialty markets or grocery stores which carry a lot of specialty food items.

Or, for the more an ambitious chefs among you, you can make the shells from scratch. I have provided a recipe. You'll need to purchase Cannoli forms (also called shells) which are a stainless steel tube around which you wrap the dough for frying. These can be purchased in most kitchen stores or on-line.

12 Cannoli

Cannoli Shell Ingredients:
(see note above)

1-1/2 cup all purpose flour

1 tablespoon granulated sugar

1/8 teaspoon salt

1 teaspoon unsweetened cocoa powder

1/4 teaspoon cinnamon (optional)

2 tablespoons butter - room temp

1 egg - separated

1/4 cup Limoncello or white wine

1 quart canola or vegetable oil (for frying)

Filling Ingredients:

1 pound ricotta cheese

3/4 cup powdered sugar

3 ounces 'mini' semi-sweet chocolate chips

Candied orange peel from one large orange, or candied citron (see Frankie's Tips)

1 tablespoon vanilla

1 egg white - beaten (optional)

Preparing Candied Orange Peel (optional):

1. Whisk 1 cup of sugar and 1/2 cup water in a medium sauce pan over medium heat. Bring to low boil.

2. Peel orange and place the chunks of rind into the sugar water. Reduce heat to low and allow to simmer.

3. Cook until orange peel is soft and almost crystallized - about a 45 minutes (add additional warm water as needed to maintain a thick syrup consistency).

4. Remove peeling with a slotted spoon and place on an un-lined plate. After cooling, chop into small pieces (about the size of chocolate chips).

Preparing Filling and Completing Cannoli:

1. Place Rictotta in a mesh strainer and sit over a bowl in the refrigerator. Allow to drain 20 to 30 minutes.

2. Place drained ricotta in a large bowl. Stir in all remaining ingredients.

3. Spoon filling into a pastry bag fitted with a large tip. Pipe filling into cooled Cannoli shells.

4. See Frankie's Tips for garnishing ideas.

Preparing the Cannoli Shells:

1. Add flour, granulated sugar, salt, cocoa powder, and cinnamon to a food processor. Process briefly.

Continued on next page

2. Add butter and the egg yolk and process briefly to incorporate. Add Limoncello (or wine) and process for 30 seconds. Stop the processor and feel the dough. It should adhere together when squeezed between your fingers (but not feel too wet or sticky). If the mixture has not begun to come together - gradually add a little cold water, 1 teaspoon at a time, and continue to process in short intervals until the mixture just begins to come together as a ball.

3. Remove mixture from processor and place on a lightly floured work surface. Knead with the ball of your hand, turning and folding several times, until the dough is smooth and elastic. Press into a ball about one inch thick. Place in a plastic bag, or wrap with plastic wrap, and refrigerate for 30 minutes (you can prepare and set aside cannoli filling during this time).

4. Unwrap dough and divide into four pieces. Re-wrap 3 remaining pieces until needed.

5. On lightly floured surface, roll out dough until it is about 1/16-inch thick (or use a pasta rolling machine). Using a cookie cutter or a sharp knife, cut dough into 4-inch circles. With rolling pin, elongate the circles into ovals.

6. Wrap the ovals lengthwise around the metal cannoli tubes. Using your fingertips, seal the overlapping edges with egg whites (see Frankie's Tips).

7. Heat oil to approximately 375° F. Gently drop shells into hot oil (2 to 3 at a time) and fry until medium-golden brown, about 2-3 minutes. Remove with tongs or a slotted spoon and drain on paper towels.

8. When the cannoli are cool enough to touch, gently twist away the molds from the shells.

Frankie's Tips:

♦ If you are making your own shells, there are a few things to be aware of. First, you want the dough to be slightly dry and fragile, somewhat like a pastry dough. Be careful not to add too much liquid.

♦ You can use either a rolling pin or a pasta rolling machine to roll out dough. If using a pasta roller, do not roll the dough out to it's thinnest setting. Stop about two settings shy, and then after cutting in circles, use a rolling pin to thin out more and form an oval.

♦ When applying egg white to the shells (step #6), you need to be extremely careful not to get any of the egg on the metal form, or your cannoli shells will stick to the form!

♦ When frying the shells, you need to maintain your oil at least an inch deep. Do not use too wide of a pan or you will need additional oil to maintain that level.

♦ It is desirable to have a thermometer which attaches to the side of the pan to check the oil temperature. Otherwise check the temperature with a stem thermometer.

♦ As far as the filling, the candied orange peel is exceptional, but if you want to simplify, use orange zest instead and add additional powdered sugar. You will give up some of the texture in the process though. Another option is to purchase citron (candied citrus fruit) at an Italian specialty store.

♦ For garnishing the cannoli, consider the following (both are shown in photo)...

♦ Slice Maraschino cherries in half and place one in either end, and then sprinkle powdered sugar over the top.

♦ My favorite is to dip the shells in chocolate and chopped pistachio nuts. Place 4 ounces of semi-sweet chocolate and a tablespoon of butter in a small glass bowl. Microwave in 20 second increments to melt. Dip the shells in the chocolate and sprinkle with chopped nuts before the chocolate sets.

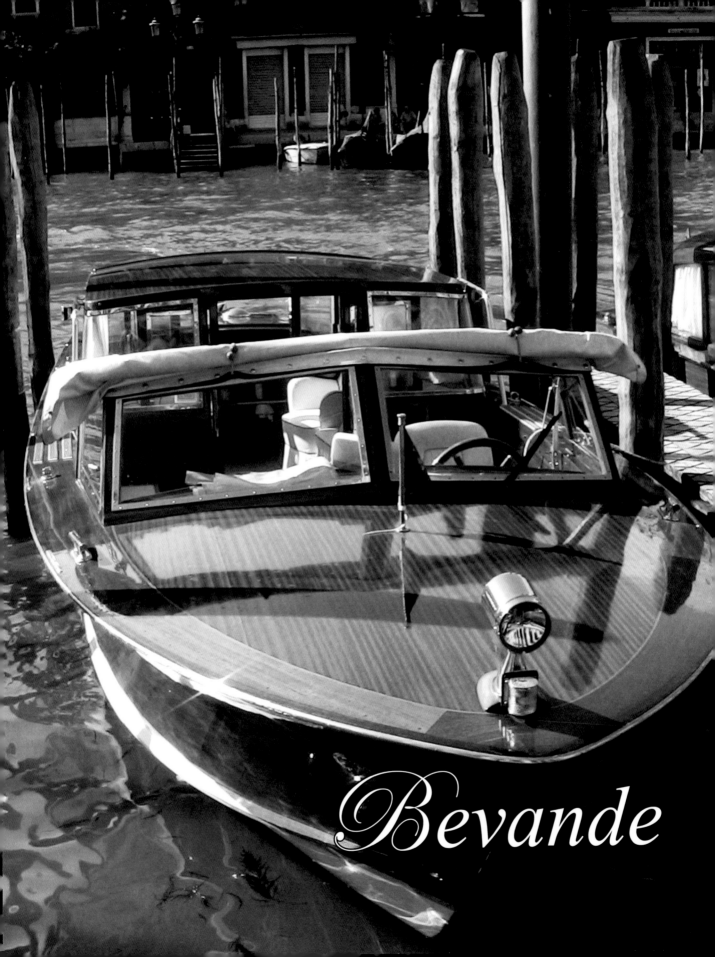

Bevande

Limoncello

Limoncello is a lemon liqueur which is primarily produced in the southern coastal areas of Italy, such as the gulf of Naples and the Amalfi Coast. It is made from fresh Lemon rinds, alcohol, water and sugar. Traditionally it is served chilled (from the freezer) as an after dinner digestivo.

Limoncello is simple to make; however it needs time to steep properly. Recipes I've worked with vary widely in how long to steep the lemons in the Vodka, and then again after the simple syrup (of sugar and water) is added. Essentially, the longer it steeps, the better it will be; yet you hit a point of diminishing return, where the differences are so subtle it is hard to even differentiate.

In addition to the ingredients listed below you will need a large glass jar, such as you would use to make sun tea. You will also need enough clear, sealable glass bottles to accommodate nearly 8 cups (about 1800 ml) of finished Limoncello. In my experience, World Market is a good place to find both the glass jar and the small bottles.

Makes about a half gallon

8 lemons

1 bottle (750 ml) Vodka

2 cups sugar

2-1/2 cups water (filtered or distilled)

1. Wash and rinse glass jar thoroughly.

2. Unless you are using organic lemons, wash them with produce wash or soap to remove any residue of pesticides or wax. Dry with a clean towel.

3. Using a vegetable peeler, remove the peel from the lemons in long strips, being careful not to get an excessive amount of the white pith. Save the lemons for another use (such as making fresh squeezed lemonade—yum!).

4. Place the peels in glass jar and pour the Vodka over the peels. Seal the jar and place in a dark, cool room temperature spot for at least 10 days (or up to 30 days).

5. After the initial 10 to 30 day period, make the simple syrup by combining sugar and water in a large sauce pan. Bring to a boil. Reduce heat and simmer about 5 minutes to thicken slightly.

6. Cool syrup completely, then pour into the Vodka mixture.

   Note: If using a shorter steeping period, leave the lemon peels in for the next phase. If using periods of more than 15 days, remove them at this time.

7. Allow to rest an additional 10 to 30 days.

8. After the rest period, remove the lemon peels and strain the Limoncello by placing a coffee filter in a mesh strainer and pouring the mixture through it into a clean pitcher. Pour from pitcher into bottles, leaving a half inch or so unfilled for expansion. Store the bottles in the freezer. Enjoy!

Positano, in Campania

Frankie's Tips:

♦ The reason you want a minimal amount of the white pith (which is the layer under the rind of the lemon), is because it will make your Limoncello bitter. A good sharp peeler is a must!

♦ This recipe is easy to double, and if you have a one gallon jar, it will just accommodate a double batch. Because of the alcohol, and since held in the freezer, it will last forever (well almost).

♦ Many recipes downplay the importance of using a high quality Vodka, and their results speak for themselves with a rough tasting Limoncello. Good Vodkas can be very expensive though. My local liquor store recommended the Vikingfjord brand to me. It costs about a third compared to the most highly reputed, but I was very happy with the results.

♦ Some recipes call for using Everclear, which is similar too Vodka but higher proof (95% alcohol / 180 Proof); or using one bottle of Vodka and one Everclear (for a double batch). One reason for this is to ensure it will not freeze in the freezer. Feel free to do so, though personally I don't like my Limoncello quite so strong. I've had great results with the Vodka. It might freeze up slightly, depending on just how cold your freezer is, but will thaw very quickly.

♦ A good friend of ours made a batch of Limoncello in which she placed Lavender during the steeping period. It was very good—so if you are adventurous, give it a whirl. I chose to follow tradition.

Brad's Bellinis

My friend Brad Cecil made Bellinis for a cook book party hosted in their home. I enjoyed them so much I asked if I could put the recipe in my cook book. Happily he agreed!

The Bellini has a colorful history. It was invented back in the 1940's by Giuseppe Cipriani, founder of Harry's Bar in Venice, a favorite haunt of Ernest Hemingway, Sinclair Lewis and Orson Welles

The original recipe was made with a puree of white peaches with Prosecco (a sparkling Italian white wine), and a touch of raspberry juice for color. Brad has given me both a "Quick Recipe", made with Peach Schnapps; and a "Traditional Recipe", which would be delicious with fresh summer peaches.

Quick recipe quantities are per drink

Quick Recipe:

1 part Peach Schnapps (or canned peach nectar)

dash of raspberry puree or Grenadine

1/2 tablespoon peach nectar (optional)

3 parts chilled Prosecco wine

Traditional recipe serves 6

Traditional Recipe:

2/3 cup fresh white peach puree (see procedure at right)

1 teaspoon raspberry puree

1 bottle chilled Prosecco wine

Quick Recipe:

1. Fill champagne flute 1/4 way with Peach Schnapps.
2. Add raspberry puree (or Grenadine), and peach nectar.
3. Top off with chilled prosecco wine.

Traditional Recipe:

1. Peel fresh peaches. Cut into pieces and puree in food processor (see Frankie's Tips)
2. For raspberry puree, place fresh or frozen raspberries (thawed) in food processor and puree.
3. Place 1-1/2 tablespoon of peach puree in the bottom of each flute.
4. Add a few drops of raspberry puree.
5. Top off with chilled Prosecco wine.

Frankie and Brad's Tips:

- For the Traditional recipe, I've not had the opportunity to test to see how many peaches are needed to achieve the 2/3 cup of puree. My guess is 2 good size peaches should be plenty. If you cannot find white peaches, yellow will work fine.

- Same with the raspberries, but if it were me I'd just do a lot and use the remaining puree for other purposes (or make Bellinis every night)!

- Brad says he sometimes substitutes a raspberry or loganberry liqueur for the raspberry puree.

Frankie's "All Natural" Italian Sodas
and Cremosas

When I decided to put Italian Sodas in the book, I wanted to do something different. So I decided to make my syrups from fresh fruit and sweeten it with honey and raw sugar. Typically, Italian Sodas are made by mixing espresso syrups with carbonated water. Espresso syrups are very sugary and I felt I could achieve something both healthier and better tasting by making the syrups myself. I was right!

A cremosa is simply an Italian Soda with a little half & half added. To continue the healthy theme, I decided to try some light coconut milk instead. This works especially well with the Mango syrup, since it already has a tropical flavor anyway.

So here is something that your kids will love (grown up kids too). And they are nutritious as well!

2 Liters of soda water and one syrup recipe will yield 6 Italian sodas

Mango Syrup:

8 ounces Mango--fresh or frozen (and thawed)

1/2 cup water

1/2 cup honey

1/2 cup raw sugar (preferably organic)

Berry Syrups:

12 ounces berries--fresh or frozen (and thawed)

3 ounces water

1/2 cup honey

1/2 cup raw sugar (preferably organic)

Other ingredients:

All Natural Sparkling Mineral Water

Light Coconut milk or Half & Half (optional)

Whipped cream (if you want to be decadent)

Mango Syrup:

1. Puree mango in a blender or food processor.
2. Place Mango in pan over low heat with water, honey and sugar. Heat, stirring regularly until sugar dissolves.
3. Cool and place in a covered container until needed.

Berry Syrups:

1. Place berries in a pan over low heat with the water, honey and sugar. Mash berries with a potato masher. Heat, stirring regularly until sugar dissolves.
2. Using a rubber spatula, press berry mixture through a strainer to remove seeds and pulp (consider saving these for another use such as smoothies).
3. Cool syrup. Place in a covered container until needed.

Italian Sodas and Cremosas:

1. Place two fingers or more of syrup in bottom of glass.
2. Add mineral water and ice. Stir. Adjust quantity of syrup to taste. Garnish with fresh fruit if desired.
3. If making a Cremosa, add Light Coconut milk or Half & Half. Let it sink down on it's own. If you want to be decadent, add some whipped cream.

Frankie's Tips:

♦ Okay, now you've got the idea. Experiment with other fruit to create your own concoctions.

Blueberry Cremosa, Mango Cremosa with Whipped Cream, Raspberry Italian Soda

Index

The two oil paintings at left are original works created by me (Frankie). I have placed them throughout the book to indicate recommended wine pairings.

The top painting is shown whenever the recommended wine is an Italian white wine. The bottom whenever the recommendation is an Italian red.

I hope you will search out some of these recommended wines. I truly believe you will enjoy them!

And now I leave you with my favorite Italian toast...

"May we all die young (pause), as late as possible!"

Ciao and Buon Appetitio!

Italian Red & Rosé Wine Index:

Italian White Wine Index:

The tiny hill town of Castelnuovo dell'Abate near Montalcino, Tuscany